Invisible Threads

INVISIBLE THREADS

MARGUERITE MacCURTIN

BEEHIVE

Published 2022 by
Beehive Books
7–8 Lower Abbey Street
Dublin 1
Ireland
info@beehivebooks.ie
www.beehivebooks.ie

Beehive Books is an imprint of Veritas Publications.

ISBN 978 1 80097 041 0

10 9 8 7 6 5 4 3 2 1

Lines from 'The Waste Land' by T.S. Eliot from *The Waste Land and Other Poems* (Faber and Faber, 1972). Lines from 'Seeing Things' by Seamus Heaney from *Opened Ground: Selected Poems, 1966–1996* (Faber and Faber, 1998). Used with permission.

A catalogue record for this book is available from the British Library.

Designed by Clare Meredith, Beehive Books
Cover design by Padraig McCormack, Beehive Books
Printed in the Republic of Ireland by Walsh Colour Print, Kerry

Beehive Books is a member of Publishing Ireland.

Beehive books are printed on paper made from the wood pulp of managed forests.
For every tree felled, at least one tree is planted, thereby renewing natural resources.

To Frank, the keystone of my life.

CONTENTS

FOREWORD

MARGUERITE MACCURTIN WOULD DRINK TEA FOR IRELAND. You'll discover, as you read, that it's not just ordinary tea but also ... *yak butter tea*!

She'll talk to you animatedly about her travels, but only if she senses you are really interested. She'll also, if you'd like, talk with passion about art, fabrics, buildings, people, paintings, colours, religion and politics – and talk till the cows come home.

She'll then ask if you'd like more tea.

When I mention to her what the tailor Timothy Buckley, of *The Tailor and Ansty* fame, had once said of people who, in his opinion, were rushing about on trains and aeroplanes to visit faraway places, that the man who knows his own doorstep already knows a great deal about the world, she responds instantly that the tailor was absolutely right.

In fact, ask her about rural Galway or Inishbofin and stand by for entertaining and detailed word-pictures from her lived experiences.

Her accounts of travels and wanderings into distant lands may suggest to you that perhaps she's on some personal pilgrimage of discovery. And just like the *Canterbury Tales*, her pilgrimage is also rich with stories.

Indeed, I can't hear the opening words of Shelley's poem 'Ozymandias' without Marguerite springing to mind: 'I met a traveller from an antique land, | Who said ...' – because that's where her storytelling takes off.

Tim Lehane
Former RTÉ Radio 1 producer and presenter

ACKNOWLEDGEMENTS

MY WRITING JOURNEY BEGAN IN 1986 WITH AN INVITATION, a commission and a letter of encouragement. These three things happened simultaneously. Gay Byrne invited me to speak about my travels on the *Late Late Show*; Howard Kinley, features editor with the *Irish Times*, commissioned me to write a series of five articles for their travel section; and Eddie McParland, one of my inspirational teachers in the Department of History of Art and Architecture at Trinity College Dublin, sent me a letter of encouragement urging me to keep writing. I am greatly indebted to each one of them.

A massive thank you to Gráinne Putney, my collaborator, neighbour and friend, without whom *Invisible Threads* would have unravelled a long time ago.

Enormous thanks to the inimitable Síne Quinn, who is the midwife of this book. Without her vision it would have never seen the light of day. Thank you also to my editor, David Macken, who has to be the most rigorous, patient and unflappable man in the publishing world, and to Clare Meredith, Padraig McCormack and all the team at Beehive Books for producing such a beautiful book.

A huge thanks to Kathleen Watkins for her guidance, insights and invaluable advice.

A very warm thank you to Anne Friel for her unwavering belief and encouragement.

A special thank you to Fionnuala Brennan for initially introducing me to Síne Quinn and for her many efforts on my behalf.

I would like to acknowledge the endless support that I received from Mary Quigley and Fr John Feighery over the years. They left no stone unturned.

My warmest thanks to Rachel Murphy for granting me permission to use Dervla Murphy's generous endorsement of my work.

Thank you to Terry Prone for suggesting that I should send my travel stories to *Sunday Miscellany* on RTÉ 1.

My broadcasting career was initially fostered by Martha McCarron on *Sunday Miscellany* and developed by Tim Lehane, producer of *Another Time, Another Space* who taught me how to 'fly' on radio. Warmest thanks to Martha and Tim.

A big thank you to Marie Heaney for including 'A Morning with an Oracle' in two *Sunday Miscellany* anthologies and for her constant encouragement and support.

Thank you also to Máire Nic Gearailt for featuring my travel stories in her *Quiet Quarter* slot on RTÉ Lyric FM and many thanks to Máire and Eoin Brady for including my stories in two *Quiet Quarter* anthologies.

Thank you to Clíodhna Ní Anluain for including 'An Easter Journey, 1916' in her *Sunday Miscellany* anthology. Many thanks to Sarah Binchy for featuring 'The Letter' on *Sunday Miscellany* on RTÉ 1.

Thank you to Ruth Buchanan for frequently featuring excerpts from my travel stories, produced by Tim Lehane, on *Playback* on RTÉ Radio 1.

Acknowledgements

A very big thank you to the many people who played an important role in my writing world. These include: Laura Kuckes, Maura Teissier, Professor Lauro Martines, Julia O'Faoiláin, Molly Marriner, Susana Walton, Yvonne Cochrane, Alessandra Vinciquerra, Dmitry Tereschenko, Hannemarie Wirtz, Robert O'Byrne, Margaret Lee, Maura Connolly, Mary O'Sullivan, Patrick Mason, Tony Flannery, Marguerite van Geldermalsen, Mohammed Othman, Roberto Baguzzi, Stephen Lushington and Beatrice Roethke.

A heartfelt thank you also to all my dear friends – you know who you are.

Finally, a loving thank you to my very precious and amazing family and extended family. Your unconditional love has taught me the true essence of life.

INTRODUCTION

I AM A NATURAL NOMAD. THE CALL OF THE WILD IS DEEP IN MY DNA.

My first planned trip was to fly to visit the man in the moon. I was four. My mother kitted me out with paper wings and provisions. She packed my bag with chocolate, biscuits, fruit and fizzy orange. I said goodbye to my parents and my brother Seán and set off down the long garden path towards the forest and waited.

Sadly, I didn't get lift-off.

My next attempt at flying was at Carnmore Airport in Co. Galway. I joined the flying club there. The club house was a single-decker bus collapsed onto the grass verge opposite the hanger. The control tower was a bungalow with no view of anything except the side of the hanger. The runway was a narrow strip down the centre of a field surrounded by stone walls. My flying instructor was the legendary Mick Farragher. When Mick decided that I was fit to fly solo he got out of the single-engine Rallye plane, looked at me in the pilot's seat and said: 'I don't often pray, but I'm going to pray now.'

However, I had the rare distinction of having my student pilot's license temporarily revoked a few months later, because when I was coming in to land, on another solo flight, I addressed the ex-RAF captain of the Aran Islands commuter plane in very colourful non-aviation speak. The polite version is that I told him I would cut the nose of his plane off if he taxied one inch closer to the runway.

I landed. He took off.

Later he phoned my brother Seán, a qualified commercial pilot and flying instructor, and told him that he'd had an encounter with his sister at Carnmore Airport. He said he was not impressed with me, my flying skills or my language. In fact, he said language like mine had not been heard over the aviation airwaves since the Second World War.

I abandoned the skies for a career in fashion. For a decade I worked four jobs simultaneously. I was modelling, styling and lecturing in Ireland and working as a marketing director for a French ready-to-wear company based in Paris.

I spent a third of my year travelling for work. In 1986 the Paris company closed, so I decided to take a break for a few months and have a look at the world beyond Europe and the United States. My bucket list included sailing up the Nile in Egypt on a felucca, visiting the Golden Triangle in India and trekking in Nepal.

As I was booking my trip in a well-known budget travel agency in London I saw a flier promoting the first-ever opportunity to travel overland from Kathmandu in Nepal to Lhasa in Tibet. I booked the journey. I joined a group of a dozen people in Kathmandu and we set off on a rickety bus towards the border between Nepal and Tibet. We travelled onwards, over unpaved roads at high altitudes, across the roof of the world surrounded by Himalayan landscapes rarely seen by Western travellers.

Villages in Tibet were scarce, but there were many white-washed religious shrines and endless prayer walls built of stones that had been left by pilgrims to mark their journeys. Decorative garlands of protective prayer flags in blue, green, red, yellow and white fluttered constantly in the wind.

The Tibetans are deeply religious. Pilgrimage is a central part of their lives. As we got closer to Lhasa we passed crowds of people walking and reciting the sacred Buddhist mantra 'Om mani peme hum' – 'Hail to the jewel in the lotus.' They counted their recitations on their wooden prayer beads or whirled little portable prayer wheels to propel their mantras heavenwards.

The seventh-century Jokhang Temple, situated in the old part of the city of Lhasa, is considered to be one of the holiest places in Tibet. We watched as pilgrims threw themselves on the ground before the temple in prayerful worship while others recited their mantras or burned juniper bushes to offer fragrant aromas to the gods. Close to the temple hundreds of stalls sold jumbled masses of textiles, carpets, clothes, scarves, trinkets, jewellery, prayer beads, sacred ceremonial objects, fresh mutton and yak butter for tea.

The men and women in the market were dressed in Tibetan-style clothes. The men wore woollen breeches, knee-length boots of felt or yak hide, jerkins, long sheepskin coats and hats. The women wore black, floor-length, rough-wool dresses, blouses and brightly striped aprons. They also wore turquoise and coral jewellery and threaded coloured ribbons through their black, braided hair. They were particularly fascinated by our foreign clothes, the texture of our hair and the smell of our skin. They pressed their faces against our hair, our faces, our arms and hands and giggled. It was all done in a playful and fun manner.

We were offered gifts of scarves, food and yak butter tea by the open-hearted, warm and generous traders of this medieval market. They chatted to us. We chatted to them. We hadn't a word in common except mime, gesture, facial expressions, hugs, handshakes and smiles.

My time in the monasteries with the monks and the pilgrims, and my interactions with the people in the medieval market near the Jokhang Temple, were the highlights of my first journey to Tibet. I realised that places, however spectacular, are nothing without people. It is the random encounters with the local people in countries across the globe that have informed my view of their worlds. It is their stories, their beliefs, their religious practices, their rituals and their empathic connection with the traveller in their midst that became the gossamer filaments that were finally woven into the tapestry of *Invisible Threads*.

PART ONE

HIGHS
AND LOWS

THE RED
PRAYER ROOM

I MET HIM IN KATHMANDU, THE MAN WHO CHANGED MY LIFE, in a monk's prayer room at sunset, sipping hot sweet tea. He was sitting on a crimson-coloured cushion beneath a red wall covered with brightly painted murals depicting scenes from the life of Buddha. He poured me a cup of this sweet tea and spoke in a quiet voice of a journey he had just made to Kailash, the mountainous home of the gods that lies deep in the heart of Tibet, close to the sources of the five main rivers of Asia. He had travelled for a thousand kilometres across the roof of the world, he told me, through a place so radiant that he thought he had arrived in a paradise of light. He described landscapes that glowed with the hues of precious stones and lakes of turquoise and emerald green, rivers of sapphire blue, mountains of amethyst mauve, sands of silver and gold, white pearls of ice that pierced an indigo sky and arcs of iridescent rainbows that bridged the heavens to the earth.

Darkness did not diminish the glories of this enchanted place, he recounted. In the embers of the dying day, the sun's rays burnt fires of snow across the frozen peaks of the Himalayas. Night simply drew its black-diamond cloak and a million sparkling stars danced amongst the fiery tails of comets exploding in the sky. The Milky Way unfurled and fluttered like a white veil of translucent chiffon amongst the cosmic splendours of these restless constellations. A crescent light appeared at the edge of the horizon and an alabaster moon rose to warm the world in the wash of its amber glow until dawn.

He spoke of how, in the early morning, frost crackled on the ground and the wind blew feathery plumes from the snow-capped dome of Mount Kailash. Through the cold, grey mists, blue smoke swirled upwards from damp fires boiling kettles of strong black tea. He sat amongst pilgrims swaddled in heavy sheepskin coats and hats and brightly patterned boots who fortified themselves with yak butter tea and barley-flour tsampa, a Himalayan staple, before tackling the highest pass of the three-day circuit around this majestic home of the gods. From the surrounding monasteries, the sounds of trumpets and cymbals blasted through the dawn air as monks chanted and prayed and drank yak butter tea and the Himalayas sprang to life.

The images of his story were so vivid and the sound of his voice so soothing that I didn't notice the sun had set and the light had begun to fade. He stood up suddenly and said, 'It is time for evening prayer.' I walked with him down a flight of stairs into the bustling courtyard of Swayambhunath. After the calm of the red prayer room it was a shock of frenzied activity. Bronze prayer wheels whirled. Coloured prayer flags snapped in the breeze. Voices prayed. Bells rang. Dogs barked. Monkeys chattered and jumped about. Children laughed and played. Fires smouldered. Sweet-smelling incense wafted from shrines. Sculpted deities wore garlands of scented flowers. Throngs of pilgrims circled the whitewashed dome of the great Buddhist stupa sending a chorus of incantation to the clouds. 'Om mani peme hum,' they chanted – 'Hail to the jewel in the lotus.'

The purple, oval eyes of the stupa of Swayambhunath followed us as we threaded our way towards the main prayer hall through crowds of women in glistening gold saris and men wearing trousers and brightly coloured shirts. As we drew nearer the monumental red doors, the sounds of trumpets, cymbals and horns heralded the approach of night. The man stopped, smiled, joined his hands together and said, 'I must leave you here. You have many journeys to make and far to travel yet, but always remember that those who don't merit to see the face of Mount Kailash will never succeed in their journey.'

He bowed, and we parted.

It was many years and many journeys later, long after I had eventually reached Mount Kailash, that the true impact of this chance encounter dawned on me. That was the moment that my old life slipped away and my new life began and the pattern that emerged on that evening, of insights gained, connections made and worlds revealed over a cup of tea, was to become a feature of all my future journeys.

I never met him again, the man who changed my life, although I have often searched for him on my subsequent visits to Swayambhunath. I only know that his name was Lama Kalsang and that one brief hour of listening to him as we shared a pot of tea at sunset changed the course of my life forever.

SPRING FESTIVAL
IN LADAKH

IN THE STILLNESS OF THE HIMALAYAN MOONLIT NIGHT, THE
kingdom of Ladakh crackled with the sounds of freezing icicles.
Glaciers and snow-covered peaks cast luminous shadows on an
arid landscape haunted by the spirit of a long-departed sea. From
time to time a blast of trumpet or a horn echoed through the
valleys from the many Buddhist monasteries nearby. As I listened,
I was reminded that prayer is a crucial feature of this dazzling,
mountain-locked land, which is ruled by the most violent and
unpredictable forces of nature. Ceremonies of petition and
appeasement are conducted around the clock to worship a host
of deities invested with miraculous powers of protection. Prayer
walls, prayer wheels and prayer flags are a central feature of the
landscape. Sacred places and holy shrines abound, many of which
are said to have supernatural powers that enable them to redirect
even an avalanche that threatens to destroy them.

Every day is an auspicious day devoted to the worship of
one god or another, and no chore, however trivial, is undertaken
without the appropriate prayers and blessings.

With this in mind I asked my guide, Tashi, what rituals we should observe before setting out on the long and dangerous road to Kargil, near the border with Kashmir. 'We will go to Hemis Monastery tomorrow,' he said, 'for the last day of the spring festival in honour of the god Mahakala, the preserver of life and destroyer of death.'

The next day we sat with maroon-clad monks sipping hot yak butter tea in a prayer hall dramatically decorated with painted banners, brightly coloured tiered umbrellas and hundreds of yak butter lights.

Twenty or so monks donned tall yellow hats and stoles and chanted prayers from the holy scriptures to the sounds of gongs, trumpets and horns. Rice statues of the god Mahakala, sculpted as a ferocious monster, and his consort, sculpted as a menstruating goddess with blood-filled nipples, stood before us in the middle of the floor. A monk wearing a white mouth mask anointed the statues with yak butter oil from time to time. A loud gong sounded.

The head monk, dressed in a full-length pink and blue embroidered Chinese robe and a tall hat embellished with a stack of carved gods' heads, stood up and walked towards the courtyard. The other monks followed in procession carrying the sculptures of Mahakala and his consort through the courtyard to a group of rocks beyond the gates of the monastery.

The head monk then draped the goddess with white gauze prayer scarves and embedded her in a standing position between two large stones facing away from the monastery door. The sculpture of Mahakala was then destroyed in a huge ritual brush fire fuelled with offerings of coloured blocks of wood, arrows, knives, rice sculptures, fruits of the earth, grain, oil and local beer.

On the following day we began our journey to Kargil on a narrow, winding road slung like a shelf on the edge of the mountain in a never-ending series of S-bends. Melting snow drifts laced with rock and sand grated the undercarriage of the car, making the journey almost impossible. Ten miles from Kargil the brakes failed. We crashed at speed into the curve of the bend and the car ended up on its roof with the boot hanging over the precipice some five hundred feet above the valley of the Indus River. We climbed out somehow and sat dazed on the side of the road unable to believe that we had survived.

Our bags had flown from the boot down into the river valley with the impact of the crash and were never seen again.

As I nursed my broken ribs in the ensuing weeks, I wondered what benevolent force had given us the two inches that made the difference for us between life and death.

I'll never know.

One thing, however, is certain. I have never doubted again the power of sacred shrines or holy places to reroute avalanches or other malevolent forces of nature from their destructive paths.

BETWEEN HEAVEN
AND EARTH

LADAKH IS A KINGDOM ON THE ROOF OF THE WORLD, SITUATED so close to heaven that it offers a dialogue with God.

It was the holy month of Ramadan and the eerie chanting from the mosque filled the moonlit air till dawn. These other-worldly sounds seemed to be the only constant feature of that fateful night. Everything else came and went.

Visions of mangled metal and flesh, memories of bracing myself for death, medics with stethoscopes and machines, a man in a woollen cape with sweet tea and hot water bottles, moments of terror and panic, scenes and sounds from the crash, sensations of being unable to talk or move, feelings of horror, fear, anger and joy.

The sun rose. I had passed the crisis point.

A man arrived by my bedside at midday, hugging a prayer mat and an unlit hubble-bubble pipe close to his chest. 'I am fasting for the holy month of Ramadan,' he informed me as he looked longingly at my untouched food. 'You are the first tourist in Kargil this year.'

He was the emissary of the town, sent by the people of Kargil to confirm that a fair-haired foreigner had had a miraculous escape on the much-feared road from Leh.

'You are a very lucky person,' he continued. 'Most people who crash on that road die.' He paused. 'But then death is nothing new to us. We see it every day.' His moustached mouth broke into a dazzling smile and he left as suddenly as he had arrived.

Outside my hospital window, pink almond blossoms glowed in the radiant light beamed from the white sealskin textures of the snow-covered glaciers. Poplars and willows laden with freshly formed lemon-green leaves fanned the intensively cultivated fields. The roof of the world sprang to life under lapis lazuli skies and the incomparable intensity of Ladakhi light. All morning long the animals grazed on the hillsides. Farmers sang a yodelling type of song that echoed through the valleys as they prepared the sandy terraces with lumps of dung fertiliser for tilling with yak and plough. Flocks of crows flew over the newly mown earth and the midday sun momentarily etched their gliding shadows down the sides of the opposite slopes.

A week or so later I made the return journey along the same dangerous mountain road that runs between the joint capitals of Ladakh, from Kargil, close to the Kashmiri border, to Leh. I was driven by the chief Indian roads engineer, Colonel Ghana, the man who had rescued me from the overturned car. His wife and two daughters accompanied us.

We stopped briefly to view the site of my car accident. Somewhere five hundred to a thousand feet of sheer cliff below us, my luggage, which had flown from the boot with the impact of the crash, lay amongst the skeletons of the dead trapped in the mangled remains of buses, cars and trucks.

I prayed quietly in thanksgiving for the blessing of having survived my car accident and for the people entombed in these rusting wrecks that littered the bed of the Indus River. On the spur of the moment I held my late uncle's 'sick-call' crucifix that I carried as an amulet in my waist bag and asked him for a sign. I didn't expect a reply.

Shortly afterwards, though I was still far from well, I flew from Leh to Islamabad, which was to be the starting point of a Silk Road journey I had already planned. I asked the concierge at the hotel if there was an Irish embassy there. I felt that I would like a diplomat to send an official message of thanks, on my behalf, to Colonel Ghana and the Indian army doctors and staff for their extraordinary care and kindness to an Irish stranger. I was informed that Ireland did not have an embassy in Islamabad but that there was a convent quite close to the hotel that was run by a congregation of Irish nuns.

I phoned the convent and was invited to visit the next afternoon for tea. I arrived with flowers and gifts from the local market and was shown into the hall by a young Pakistani girl. I didn't know what order of nuns ran this convent but while I was waiting I noticed the portrait of a woman whom I recognised. It was of Nano Nagle, the foundress of the Presentation Order. My beloved late uncle had purchased a copy of Nano Nagle's portrait to take back to the nuns who ran a school in his parish in Los Angeles.

The reverend mother arrived. She greeted me warmly.

'I recognise the portrait of your foundress,' I said. 'My late uncle took a copy to his parish in Los Angeles a few years ago.'

'Who was your uncle?' she asked.

'Father Aidan Day,' I replied.

'I knew him very well,' she said. 'Three of the four nuns in this convent worked in his parish. He was a close friend. Let me take you to meet them.'

I never mentioned my request for a sign, but as I looked again at Nano Nagle's portrait, I silently acknowledged my uncle's reply.

A MORNING WITH
AN ORACLE

IN THE HIMALAYAN KINGDOM OF LADAKH, THE APRIL FULL MOON
cast an icy glow over the ancient city of Leh. Its buildings, glazed
with frost and icicles, shimmered in the shadows of surrounding
glaciers.

In the dining room of a local hotel, I joined a diverse collection
of people gathered around large pots of bubbling hot food
arranged along a large rectangular table. The atmosphere was
warm and chatty until a bearded man who had been speaking
in hushed tones leapt suddenly from his chair and proceeded
to dance wildly around the centre of the room. He touched his
chin with his knees in the course of a frenetic, limb-throwing
performance. A fellow traveller informed me that he had been
miraculously cured by an oracle who was said to be possessed by
the spirit of a god. Three weeks ago, according to my friend, the
dancing man could not even walk.

The next morning I entered the crowded, smoke-filled
kitchen of the oracle's house in the nearby village of Saboo. A
tiny woman with deeply lined skin and dark hair was raised on

a stack of cushions in the corner of the kitchen. She was dressed in a red and turquoise silk cape lined with shocking pink and embroidered with Chinese cloud motifs. On her head she wore a narrow-brimmed top hat that was strewn with layers of white gauze prayer scarves. Her mouth was covered with a red triangular piece of cloth. She clutched a bell and shook it violently and then began to chant feverishly as she went into the motions of her trance. Her face became contorted, her eyeballs flicked up, her body writhed and shivered and her voice shrieked.

A deathly silence gripped the crowd. The oracle screamed for pilgrims. The crowd pushed a reluctant woman forward. She staggered half upright from her kneeling position to place an offering scarf on the oracle's hat. She fell to her knees to outline the details of her problem. The oracle emitted some high-pitched rasping and hissing sounds, removed her mask and buried her face in the exposed flesh of the woman's abdomen. She raised her face and spat a black-looking bile that she had apparently sucked from the woman's stomach without wounding her into a bowl of hot ashes that was placed nearby. Pilgrim followed pilgrim. The oracle's responses grew more frantic. Her healing methods varied only to include the use of a bamboo tube for releasing the black bile of evil from a pilgrim's neck, tongue, cheeks and abdomen.

A mother with a very sick baby knelt before her. The oracle's daughter handed her a knife that had been reddened in the fire. She placed the burning blade on her tongue until it sizzled. Then she gently blew over the head and body of the baby. Finally, she prayed over some barley and handed it to those nearest to her. She also blessed the people who knelt before her by touching them on the shoulders, head and back with the dagger and *dorje* (thunderbolt symbol), which are sacred ritual instruments of Buddhism. She came out of her trance as noisily as she had entered it and slumped in an exhausted, frail-looking bundle amongst the cushions.

The pilgrims filed from the room. I sat in silence with some local women on the smooth mud floor. Her daughter seized a bellows and fanned the yak dung fire in the great black stove. She offered large mugs of hot sweet tea to everyone in the room. We watched as the oracle folded her ceremonial clothes and placed them neatly in a box. She turned towards us and dissolved the tension that had gripped the gathering with a wide, warm smile.

She spoke to me through a Ladakhi friend who acted as an interpreter. We chatted about the hazards of mountain travel and I told her about the injuries I had sustained in a recent car accident on a treacherous road nearby. Before I left she handed me some barley and a chain of coloured threads to protect me on dangerous trails and keep bad luck at bay. In a land where paralysed men get up and dance, the westerner soon learns to adopt the natives' ways.

LUANG PRABANG

AT DAWN THE CITY OF LUANG PRABANG, FORMER ROYAL CAPITAL of Laos, was shrouded in an amethyst veil of gauzy mist, brocaded with sprays of green foliage. The small airport was nestled in a narrow valley surrounded by jungle-covered mountains that were splashed with a web of ochre-coloured streaks. These streaks were the dusty imprints of the well-worn pathways that joined the remote villages of the uplands and highlands to the more accessible valleys and the city below.

The tiny Fokker Friendship turboprop plane bumped up and down on the thermals as it began its descent, offering us the kind of aeronautical trauma that should be avoided by those with a fear of flying. The pilot headed the plane directly towards a tall peak that was blocking the approach to the runway until the plane's nose was almost flush with the rock face. At the crucial moment he banked to the right, then to the left, flying in a semicircle around the obstacle until the airport came into view. He then dropped swiftly towards the short runway, which was slung between two narrow back gardens. The wheels skimmed over flaming stoves and steaming pots of noodles before they screeched on melting rubber towards a hedge of colourful bougainvillaea. Finally, the impact of the landing brought a shower of melons and baguettes, hauled by the locals from the capital Vientiane, tumbling out of the storage bins onto our heads below.

From the Luang Prabang hotel, the royal city sprawled along the banks of the Mekong River, between coconut palms and bamboo trees, towards the surrounding chains of mountains. For the traveller, it is one of the few places in the world that has the pristine charm of a city that has preserved much of its original character intact. In the early morning the streets are filled with ruby-and-gold-clad Buddhist monks in search of food for their daily rations. With heads shaved and feet bare, they carry their black lacquer begging bowls from place to place to gather offerings of vegetables and sticky rice from the people for the two meals permitted to them each day. They eat at 7 a.m. and 11 a.m., because after midday they must fast from food, though not from drinks, until after dawn the next day.

Just after midday a boatload of monks dressed in a blaze of red and yellow robes were sailing down the mighty Mekong River beside me. Freed from their morning restraints of begging, they had adopted a more festive look by sporting large psychedelic sunglasses and wide-brimmed straw hats for the leisurely trip on the river. They were protected from the blazing sun by a circular screen of big black umbrellas.

They drew up alongside a sandbank and a tall, athletic-looking monk with spectacular strobing black and white op-art sunglasses jumped out. Puffing on a fat cheroot, which he held between his dazzling white teeth, he grabbed a jutting rock nonchalantly with one hand and the boat's mooring rope equally nonchalantly with the other. Then, with the flourish of some well-known pop star performing a grand finale, he hauled his fellow monks onto the rocks beside him. The cheroots were passed around and lit and they enthusiastically waved us on our river journey with a playful performance of blowing circles of smoke from their cheroots into the air.

Further downstream, women stood waist-deep in the water panning for gold. The guide told me that it is the men who dig the sand from the pits along the river bank in the morning and leave it ready for panning by the women in the afternoon. During my visit it was the young girls who dug and carried the shoulder baskets of sand to the water's edge while other girls panned breast-deep in the river. First they placed a couple of shovels full of sand in a basket, which was in turn placed on a wooden panning bowl and swished from side to side in the water. When the sand had been sifted, the stones were thrown onto the shore and the sand in the bowl was washed by the same swishing method until only its finest grains remained. The gold dust began to sparkle from amongst the last and finest particles. These final grains of sand and gold dust particles were finally transferred to an enamel basin and taken to another processing place where the gold particles are separated from the sand with the help of a mercury solution. If they are lucky, the gold panners could get up to a dollar's worth (about one gram) of gold a week during the short panning season from February to April before the monsoon season begins.

However, it is not a woman's adeptness at gold panning but her ability to weave fine cloth that is reputed to have the power of an aphrodisiac for the unmarried Laotian male. In the past, it is said, it definitely increased a woman's chances in the marriage stakes when excellence in this art distinguished her from her less accomplished sisters and won her the heart of her suitor.

A closer look, however, reveals that there is much more to be gleaned from Laotian fabric than its role in procuring a man. The patterns, colours and motifs are elements of a complex textile language that reveals the tribal history of the weavers and the cultural history of Laos' trade with China and the islands of Southeast Asia. As early as 2000 BC, symbols such as river dragons, scrolls, interlocking spirals, ferns, hooks, snakes and spirits spoke from skirt lengths, jackets, turbans and shawls to tell about the social, religious and political past of the wearer and her people.

I visited the women weavers of the Ban Phnom village on the outskirts of Luang Prabang late on an April afternoon. At the sound of a tourist bus they abandoned their betel nut chewing, animal feeding, harvesting, monkey nut shelling, baby nursing, husbands, houses and looms to run to the village hall with samples of their work. By the time I got inside there were about thirty women and three hundred rainbow-coloured items on display. Pleas of 'Madame, here', 'Madame, this for you', 'Madame, this nice ... only 400 kips' or similar accompanied the large quantities of textiles that were thrust at me from every angle at the same time with frenzied enthusiasm. They laughed and giggled as they draped and dressed me in things that certainly did not fit, and finally I was covered in so much fabric that I pretended to collapse on the floor.

They responded by throwing even more weavings over me before they returned to their chairs, sitting in total silence while they played the waiting game. The moment I opened my eyes they all jumped up again at once and the selling began even more feverishly than before. They had some beautiful antique wedding textiles, jackets, sarongs and shawls, as well as contemporary items such as table cloths, place mats, bed covers, skirts and scarves. I eventually staggered out laden with silk textiles I did not need but that were added to the other stacks of 'essentials' such as Buddhist begging bowls, cane hats, opium weights and ill-fitting sandals that I had acquired for the long journey home.

THE FORBIDDEN
KINGDOM

IT IS DAWN IN THE HIMALAYAS. THERE ARE SEVENTEEN PEOPLE on board the small propeller plane heading along the flanks of the Annapurna mountain range towards the long forbidden kingdom of Mustang.

The pilot seems to be flying far too near the sheer walls of ice that surround us on every side. Above us, snow-covered mountains soar five miles high to pierce the dome of cobalt blue. Wisps of cloud drift by the windows. The plane bobs up and down on the thermals. The air hostess, head bent, moves through the cabin serving sweets for comfort and cotton wool to protect our ears from the loud propeller noise.

The pilot looks anxiously at the air hostess and calls her to the cockpit. They speak. She walks halfway down and looks out the windows on both sides beneath the wings. She reports back to the captain. All the passengers are now looking out the windows on both sides. The wings are there. The wheels are attached. Everything seems to be in place.

The pilot still looks anxious. The plane shudders more strongly in a thick bank of cloud. It drops twenty feet or so in the turbulence. I grasp the seat in front of me. A Nepalese woman behind me throws her arms around my throat, pushing her prayer beads into my flesh with fear. Half strangled, I turn towards her and offer her words of comfort that I neither believe nor feel.

We have been flying for twenty-five minutes. We know that soon we will be going through the narrow passageway in the ice at fifteen thousand feet that acts as the only air portal to Mustang. We also know that many planes have perished here, their pilots unable to find this slender mountain gap. The approach is terrifying. There is no room to circle. The pilot literally drops the plane beneath the icefall of the Dhaulagiri Mountain onto the dirt airstrip in the canyon below us.

We have arrived safely in Mustang, the ancient land of Lo, home of the deepest gorge on earth. We pile out of the aircraft, a jumble of locals, tourists and luggage, into a chilly, blustery atmosphere. A freezing blast of air scatters both luggage and people. A smiling young man approaches me, his hand outstretched, and says, 'Welcome to the land of cold.'

His name was Sonam. He was to be the principle guide, or *sirdar*, for my two-week visit to this mysterious land of cold trapped between the rain shadow of the Himalayas and the wild wind currents of India and Tibet.

As we walked from the airstrip towards the nearby town of Jomsom the plane was already back in the air and fleeing at speed towards that narrow ice corridor away from the strengthening winds. It was the daily presence of this raging wind, I discovered, that dominated the life and landscape of Mustang and provided both the set and the soundtrack of our lives as we made the difficult journey along the old salt-trade route towards the medieval, walled capital of Lo Manthang.

The wind began at first light with a cold blast of air from Tibet and blew until mid-morning. Then it faded away, leaving a brief moment of stillness and a window for the first and last airplane of the day. Very soon after, the winds from the south arrived. They had risen on the hot plains of India and were sucked northwards through the breach of the gorge by the low pressure of the mountain deserts where they raged until night fell, blasting and scouring and carving and moulding everything in their path. And it was into this rising wind that we set off from Jomson a few hours later, fortified with gallons of strong sweet tea and armed with stacks of essential supplies.

On the rhythms of the wind, ripples of unexpected sounds came floating by: the sweet and delicate notes of birdsong; the thunderous echoes of teams of horses splashing through the shallow rocky pools of the gorge; the voices of people singing in the fields; the sounds of horsemen shouting, dogs barking, monks chanting and children laughing and playing.

Surrounding us on every side was the wind-sculpted backdrop of the Himalayas in all its theatrical glory – monumental glaciers, moving ice falls and soaring mountains carved into fantastical shapes and serrated walls of glowing sedimentary rock rising from the deepest gorge on earth. Juxtaposed against all this splendour, tiny nuggets of emerald and gold farmland were inlaid into pinnacled cliff bases fanned by slim, willowy trees.

We camped on that first night on the edge of the village of Kagbeni. I slept fitfully to the tremors of the earth and the loud rumbling of rockfall streaming down a mountain on the opposite side of the gorge. At dawn I woke to the blast of trumpet from a nearby monastery and a cup of hot tea from the sherpas.

After a big breakfast of porridge, omelettes and pancakes, we were once again on the road walking towards one of the most compelling signs on earth for travellers: 'Restricted Area' it read, in big capital letters.

In a dark, grim, mustard-coloured room stacked with dusty, dog-eared papers and decorated with a small, yellowing map of the world, an exhausted-looking officer carefully recorded my passport details in his ledger.

'Nationality: British,' he said.

'Irish,' I replied, pointing to the small island dot on the map.

He looked, shrugged his shoulders and said: 'Next to England. No problem then. Same. Same.'

A thousand years of Anglo-Irish history wiped out with a stroke of a pen. I walked on.

By nightfall we had reached a small hotel in a village dwarfed by the monumental mountainscape around it. We were greeted by Nima, a young woman with long, dark, plaited hair woven with red and yellow threads. She was dressed in a grey Tibetan wrap-over skirt, a rainbow-coloured apron, a wine-coloured jumper and a string of Venetian crystals that sparkled in the dark smoky kitchen. She looked unnaturally clean in a land where washing is considered a waste of precious water. Very soon her parents and friends returned filthy from the muddy fields and a trio of men from the remote area of Dolpo on a pilgrimage to Lo Manthang arrived so blackened with grime and dirt as to be barely recognisable. With the normal standards of cleanliness upheld, it was time for tea. Endless cups of yak butter tea were handed around and afterwards the Dolpo pilgrims settled down around a bottle of chang, a local alcoholic beverage.

The more they drank in the dark kitchen, the more the stories flowed. Sonam told me that they spoke of distant valleys in their faraway Dolpo that were stalked by demons and monsters and witches and ghosts. The mehti (yeti, or abominable snowman), a hairy giant with a suffocating odour, prowled nightly through these valleys in search of animal or human victims. Shadowy ravines resonated with a power so sinister that people were unable to pass through invisible walls of evil. Cliff faces shimmered with streams of blood, and flames of fire and mighty torrents of water suddenly sprung up and destroyed everything in their path. Ravenous spirits guarded the secret routes to Buddhist monasteries filled with artistic treasures so sacred and so luminous that the human eye could not behold them and those who did fell dead.

In the corner of the kitchen, little oil lamps flickered, casting dancing shadows on an altar to Buddha and protector gods. At the front door there was a raised step to prevent demons entering the house and a trap above the top lintel to catch them before they got too close. A ferocious black mastiff dog guarded the house and barked endlessly, breaking the haunting quiet of the windless moonlit night. My sleep was filled with ghostly images and eerie noises and I was never happier to see the sherpas at dawn with a large mug of bed tea and hear the gradual roar of the rising wind.

Four days later, against all odds and most of the laws of gravity, we arrived safely at the summit of the last high pass. In the valley below us lay the medieval city of Lo Manthang.

Enclosed within thirty-foot-high walls and sealed by sentinel turrets at its four corners, this cubed maze of small red and white buildings was dominated by three large red monasteries and a tall white palace. Brown kindling brushwood for fires, which was stacked around the edges of all the roof tops, accentuated the geometric squareness of the buildings while prayer flags fluttering from every corner added a Buddhist note to the scene. Behind the city a painterly, cubist mountain panorama stretched in never-ending screens of peak tips to the amethyst horizons of Tibet.

The queen of Mustang is Tibetan. Her relationship with the king is one of the great love stories in the Himalayas. Their devotion is such that when their only son and heir was killed in an accident, King Jigme Palbar Bishta chose not to marry again as custom would dictate. The title now passes to his nephew.

The queen has had to live in political exile from her country and her family since her marriage because she is Tibetan and Tibet is ruled by China.

When she was informed by my local guide that I had recently visited her home city of Shigatse and that I had also made the pilgrimage to Mount Kailash, the Tibetan home of the gods, I was invited to join her for breakfast at 7 a.m. the following morning.

The door to the white palace was opened by the queen's attendant. We climbed up through several floors on rickety wooden steps under the glassy eye of a stuffed golden mastiff on permanent guard-dog duty against the demons.

The queen's sitting room had an altar with flickering butter lamps and cabinets filled with Buddhist images. Her chair was placed on a raised platform. We sat on lower platform benches. She entered. She was a slight woman with a pale, heart-shaped face. Her black, braided hair was woven with coloured threads. She wore a Tibetan-style dress and a heavy royal-blue cardigan. She was quiet and reserved. We were served yak butter tea in delicate china cups and delicious puff pastries. The queen drank from a blue lapis lazuli and silver cup. She was keen to have first-hand news of her country and she visible relaxed when I spoke to her about her home city of Shigatse and my pilgrimage around Mount Kailash.

At the end of my visit I presented her with a primrose-coloured prayer scarf. She smiled and returned it to me by draping it across my shoulders as we parted. I added it to my collection of amulets said to be needed for protection against the hungry ghosts, evil spirits and red demons rumoured to stalk this desolate and beautiful kingdom.

We returned to Jomson on horseback a few days later. We stopped at the high pass for a last look at the forbidden kingdom and performed the customary parting ritual. We lit a fragrant fire of juniper and incense and burnt little slivers of tissue paper imprinted with a prayer and blessed by a monk in Lo Manthang. We watched as they floated like silver gossamer flecks in the wind as offerings for a safe return to Jomson. We travelled in the company of herds of goats and sheep on their way down to the lower pastures for the winter.

A week later I crossed the airstrip in the strengthening winds towards the plane with Sonam. As my luggage was loaded, he took my hands and smiled and said, 'Come back soon to the land of cold.'

JOURNEY TO
MOUNT KAILASH

THE JOURNEY TO MOUNT KAILASH, THE SNOW-DRAPED HOME OF the gods in the Tibetan Himalayas, is one of the most visually beautiful journeys in the world. It is also one of the most difficult.

There are no roads, just 850 kilometres of rutted tracks, unbridged rivers, sand dunes and frozen pasturelands. The ranges of temperature at the high altitudes of this region are so extreme that warm sand dunes lie side by side with frozen pasturelands. One can get sunburn from the blazing sunshine and frostbite from the frozen ground simultaneously while standing in the same place.

It is said that the routes to Mount Kailash are littered with the bones of pilgrims attempting to get there, and the burial sites at the base of Mount Kailash are littered with the bones of those who arrived and died.

I travelled with four others, two German women, a German man and a Japanese man, in battered Land Cruisers from Zhangmu in Nepal across the old kingdom of Ngari. We were accompanied by a guide, two drivers, a cook and a truck that carried all our food supplies and camping equipment for the two-week journey.

We survived the hazards of the trip with a lot of help from the many Tibetan people we met at intervals along this vast, almost deserted, region. They guided the Land Cruisers, with us on board, through the flooded fast-flowing rivers. They pulled us out of soggy sand dunes. They helped to repair our regular punctures and provided us with sheds to sleep in when we discovered that one of our party, a German doctor, did not pack the appropriate clothes for camping and sleeping at minus ten degrees.

On the fifth day we saw the dome-shaped, snow-covered silhouette of Mount Kailash towering above a range of spice-coloured mountains in the distance. We arrived in Darchen, the base camp for the three-day pilgrimage around the 'Mountain of the Gods', in brilliant sunshine, under cobalt-blue skies.

The next morning we began our walk. As we walked, Mount Kailash played its games of optical illusion, revealing and concealing one of its four different faces from behind the screens of adjoining mountain ridges at various intervals. When it was visible, plumes of snow floated on the winds from its icy mantle in gentle feathery ripples creating tremors of movement around its otherwise stately pose.

On the first night we camped in view of its north and most dramatic face. It glowed like a snow-kissed pyramid of burning embers in the alabaster light of the full moon.

The following morning we passed Shiwal Tsal, the place of ritual death, and left the customary piece of clothing here as a memento before walking on to the highest pass of 18,600 feet, to be climbed without oxygen. Here, legend says, the pilgrim is reborn.

We were joined on this pass by a Tibetan man called 'Thursday Moon, A Thousand Stars'. He pointed out burial sites filled with the bones of the dead that were left for sky burial, and the mounds of clothes and possessions that were left along the ritual route by the pilgrims for good fortune. He told us stories of the struggle between Gesar, the king of good, and Ghokar, the king of evil. Good always won, he said, as he pointed out the rocky landmarks that represented the liver, intestines and limbs of the defeated king of evil.

We left Mount Kailash four days later and walked in the frozen waters of the holy lake Mansarovar close by. A couple of days' drive from there, on the thirteenth day of our journey, we arrived at a remote homestead on the high Tibetan plateau late in the afternoon to seek shelter for the night. A tall Tibetan woman approached us. She was dressed in a Tibetan-style costume and her dark hair was tied into a long plait and decorated with coloured threads. Unfortunately, there were no rooms available in her home for that night, she told us, but she had a sheep shed she was willing to give to us. Her family would clear out the sheep and the bales of wool and we could spend the night there.

I find the oily smell of sheep and wool nauseating and, although we had all slept in abattoirs and rat-infested rooms during the journey, I just could not bear the thought of spending the night with four other people in that stinking shed. I went into the yard and sat on a pile of yak dung beneath a prayer-flag pole while the sheep shed was being cleared. The red, green, yellow, white and blue prayer flags snapped in the biting wind and the piercing cold stung my eyes so fiercely that I cried with pain.

After a short time the tall Tibetan woman and owner of the house, whose name I learned was Tsering Tensing, came towards me, took my hands and led me into her warm kitchen. Within, close to the door, there was a stove with a yak dung fire, on which stood a large pot of boiling yak butter tea. A young boy and a man sat by the stove on benches covered with Tibetan rugs. At the far end of the kitchen there was a large shrine to Buddha with many images and yak butter lights in full blaze. An old woman dressed in black with grey hair and no teeth sat by the shrine talking animatedly to me and wagging her finger as she spoke.

Tsering placed me on a bench closest to the fire. The man, who was her husband, sat on one side of me and held cups of hot yak butter tea to my lips, which I drank. The little boy, her son, sat on the other side of me and wiped my tears with his soot-blackened hands. Tsering held my hands and spoke to me, in a soft voice, words that I did not understand. The old woman continued her monologue, wagging her index finger constantly in my direction. This scenario continued for a while until my eyes began to sting from the soot and the smoke.

I took a mirror and a tissue from my wash bag, and when I saw how ridiculous I looked with my red swollen eyes and my tear-stained, soot-covered face, I started to laugh. The others looked at themselves in the mirror and laughed also. The old woman stood up and smiled and wagged her finger at me and talked even faster than before. I suppose that she was telling me to pull myself together and stop crying and get on with it. I did just that. Tsering held my hands again and her husband placed the yak butter tea to my lips and her son sat and smiled.

Later I realised that this was the most powerful moment of the journey for me. Here I was, a stranger who had wandered in from the Tibetan plateau in need of shelter and comfort and I was offered both in abundance. We had no word in common, but without the benefit of language, it is the non-verbals that click into place: body language, gesture, mime, eye contact, facial expressions, basic intuition. The condition of being human is universal, I discovered, and the underlying impulse to reach out and connect transcends the barriers of race, language, culture and geographical location.

PART TWO

BLESSINGS AND CELEBRATIONS

EASTER BENEATH THE SOUTHERN CROSS

ON SPY WEDNESDAY I ARRIVED ON THE OUTSKIRTS OF THE Peruvian city of Arequipa, situated in the long shadows of the snow-tipped volcano of Mount Misti.

Crowds of women in bowler hats and rainbow-coloured shawls had gathered to boil bags of eggs and half-feathered chickens in the bubbling waters of the many volcanic springs. Men bathed in the hot baths nearby while children splashed and played as they waited for the food to cook.

Towards sunset, the crowd departed for the town square. Here preparations for the pageants to commemorate the Christian festival of Easter were underway. The main event that evening was a procession to mark the biblical story of Christ being questioned by Pontius Pilate. A painted image of the trial scene, mounted on an ornately carved and gilded bier, was carried by stewards of the church from the Catholic cathedral through the main streets. A statue of the tragic-looking Virgin, Christ's mother, dressed in a long black velvet cape and clutching a black lace hankie to dry her wax tears, followed on a plainer bier. The procession marched in prayerful solemnity towards the town hall followed by a carnival of people carrying lighted candles. On the fringes of the crowd, toffee-apple vendors, street sellers and general merchants lost no time in plying their wares between the hymn singing and the prayers.

On Holy Thursday I made the fourteen-hour bus journey from Arequipa to Puno on the shores of Lake Titicaca. We travelled on an unpaved track across the rugged but spectacular beauty of the vast Andean Altiplano and arrived to find the town deserted in favour of Easter ceremonies in the local church.

The next morning, Good Friday, I joined a stream of people making a pilgrimage to the hillside Calvary that overlooks the town. We stopped at the ritual sites to honour the fourteen stations of Christ's journey to his crucifixion. At three o'clock, the traditionally accepted time of Christ's death, most of the people of Puno seemed to be gathered in prayer around the base of the cross.

Afterwards the people moved in groups to visit the sacred stone burial towers of their Inca ancestors situated nearby on the edge of the peninsula within sight of the Calvary monument. When darkness fell and the southern cross sat low in the moonlit sky, the last of the pilgrims filed homewards. They left the sacred shrines of the Incas and the Christian crucifixion and returned to their homes that were decorated with a similar mixture of Christian and pagan symbols. All the spirits had been accommodated and the Easter Vigil had begun.

On Easter Saturday I crossed Lake Titicaca by ferry into Bolivia and travelled by bus to La Paz, the highest capital city in the world. That evening I visited the witchcraft market close to the cathedral. Here, Aymara women in a swirl of bowler hats; wide, circular skirts and rainbow-patterned shawls tempted me with an exotic range of merchandise. Amongst the goods on display were selections of substances, amulets and instruments essential for placating capricious pagan spirits of earth and sky, as well as an endless variety of charms and herbal remedies. Under great pressure from a stall vendor, and perhaps a touch of altitude madness, I bought a Llama foetus wrapped in coloured threads that she told me would ensure good fortune if I were to bury it in the garden of my home.

On Easter Sunday I attended Mass in the Catholic cathedral of La Paz. The Easter Vigil was over and the crowds had gathered to celebrate Christ's resurrection from the dead. I stood beside the Aymara woman who had sold me the Llama foetus from her witchcraft stall the previous evening. On the other side of me in the pew, a distraught lady held a plastic effigy of the severed, bleeding, thorn-crowned head of Christ impaled on a stick close to her face and wept. The bell rang for the consecration. The white flowers glistened under the altar lights and flickering candle flames. The white-vested priest raised the circular communion bread to the heavens and the congregation bowed their heads to the ground. The stall vendor placed a tiny white chalk amulet of lovers wrapped in coloured threads into my hand and smiled. This is an amulet to attract a husband. I was already married, so I gave it to a friend. She found a husband a year or so later.

The Llama foetus also served me well, though I do wonder what archaeologists in the future will make of its remains lying snugly wrapped in Alpaca fibres under a cherry tree in Dublin.

THE PALIO FESTIVAL
OF SIENA

THE PALIO, ONE OF THE MOST INTRIGUING FESTIVALS IN ITALY, is held in the Tuscan city of Siena, Italy, on 2 July and 16 August every year in honour of two important Marian feast days dedicated to the Madonna of Provenzano and the Madonna of the Assumption, who is regarded as queen and patron of the city.

The festival is held in the same square, surrounded by the same buildings, and organised according to much the same formula as it was in the Middle Ages. It involves a lavish pageant in medieval costume followed by a ninety-second horse race of three laps by ten horses and jockeys riding bareback around the perimeter of the main square.

The name Palio comes from the Latin *pallium*, a hand-painted banner affectionately known as 'the rag', which was and still is the prize for winning the race.

On the surface it looks like a perfectly simple event. In reality it is a highly complex metaphor for the entire political, religious and social structure that, for the Senese, defines their history and sense of identity.

To try to understand it you have to become part of it, I was told. I was fortunate enough to be invited by my friend Ruth Alboretti to one of the traditional celebratory dinners that take place on the eve of the Palio. We joined the people of the Eagle district, one of the seventeen districts, or *contrade*, as they are known, that are eligible to run a horse in the race.

Horses are drawn by lot as only ten are allowed to run in the Palio, and the horse of the Eagle district was amongst those chosen, so the mood on that evening was one of great jubilation and joy.

Before dinner our hosts gave all of their guests a gift of a large, yellow, square scarf printed with the image of a double-headed eagle, elegantly framed by narrow, fluttering hands of black and cobalt-blue stripes. We learned that we were required to always wear this scarf in public over the next couple of days as a sign of our allegiance to the Eagle district. In the course of the dinner we stood frequently at the bidding of our host to toast the health of our horse and of our jockey and to pray for their success in the race the next day.

The food arrived in endless platters piled high with pastas and salads and meats and fish and cheese and fruit. The wine flowed. The more the wine flowed, the more our collective spirits rose. The more our spirits rose, the more we toasted our horse and our jockey. Occasionally, a low whisper spread throughout the table that told of plots and dirty tricks and foul play and dangers that lay ahead. The rumours grew with the hours; so much so that by midnight Ruth and I felt really afraid that before dawn our newly adopted horse and jockey would almost certainly be injured, or poisoned, or both!

They survived.

Around the time they were being blessed in the church of the Eagle district, we went with two other friends to a window in a room on the third floor of a palazzo overlooking the starting point of the race. Every building around the square was festooned with a colourful array of silks and banners and paintings and tapestries. The bells of the tower beside the castellated town hall rang constantly. Crowds of people in rainbow-coloured tops, hats and t-shirts streamed into the shell-shaped centre of the square until there was breathing room only.

In the surrounding buildings every window, every balcony and every viewing stand was crammed to capacity. Between the viewing stands and the centre of the square, a race track had been made during the previous days by compacting tons of volcanic earth, or *tufo*, which is of the reddish-brown colour that we have come to know as burnt sienna.

The pageant began with a burst of firecracker and was led by a platoon of carabinieri (police) on horseback. This was followed by a two-hour procession of different groups in sumptuous medieval costumes: velvets and furs, doublets and hose, caps and capes, hats and wigs, belts and boots, helmets and shields, and swords and spears. Nobles, knights, officers, soldiers, pages, grooms, flag-throwers, standard-bearers, footmen, crossbowmen, archers, drummers, trumpet players; they were all there and many, many more besides. A triumphal wagon pulled by four white oxen carried the Palio banner, that coveted prize for winning the race. The most moving moment of all was the parade of the ten horses with their jockeys and grooms and attendants.

And then there was silence. The music stopped. The bells stopped ringing. The track was cleared. The crowd went quiet. People fainted in the square. Bodies were passed on a scaffolding of hands through the crowd to waiting stretchers lingering dangerously on the edge of the track. A burst of firecracker again. The air was filled with a deafening roar of cheering. A sea of waving hands thrust upwards in supplication towards the heavens as the horses made their way in the stifling heat towards the starting point. There, just beneath us, we saw them jostle for position, pushing, prancing, kicking, biting, crushing against each other. Jockeys doing last-minute deals with each other, breaking away from the starting order or trying to control their nervous mounts. Each carried a crop and wore an iron helmet to protect his head from his opponent's crop.

The first start was cancelled. The jockeys vied for position again. The second start was also cancelled. The crowd screamed hysterically. Five times the start was cancelled. The crowd was almost apoplectic by this point. Finally, the rope dropped, the drums rolled, the horses raced and frenzied voices of the crowd reached deafening proportions, shouting prayers, insults, threats – 'Kill him, kill him!'; 'Murder him!'; 'Sell out!'; 'Fix! Fix!'; 'Coward!'; 'Madonna! Madonna protect him!'

On the dirt track below us, the ten horses fought for victory. They were travelling at a speed too fast for the eye to catch anything but a blur of images. Rider and horse, hoof and leg, body and hand, track and square, people and buildings all merged into a visual tangle of textures and shapes and colours and forms and then it was over. Jockeys were pulled from their horses and spirited away for their own safety. People jumped over the barriers and were trampled on. Ambulances collected the injured near the starting post. People fell to their knees, people wept, people danced, people screamed with joy. The horse of the Goose district had won.

The next day, we donned our Eagle scarves again in support of the vanquished and sat sipping tea at a cafe in the almost deserted square. We watched men from the winning side roaming around, naked to the waist, dressed only in large babies' diapers with babies' bottles full of milk and babies' soothers stuck into the sides of their mouths. When they saw our scarves they waved their bottles and soothers at us and taunted us for losing.

We responded by shouting 'Fix! Fix! Sell out! Sell out!' and other more unsavoury insults that we had learned the previous day. They departed.

'Do you know why grown men masquerading as babies ramble around the streets of Siena?' I asked my friend Ruth.

'Sometimes,' she said quietly, 'perhaps it's better not to know.'

TEMPLE OF
THE SUN

THE PHLEGRAEAN (OR FIERY) FIELDS FABLED IN THE STORIES
of early classical civilisation lie north-west of the city of Naples
in Southern Italy. Here, at a place called Cumae, on the spur of
a hillside surrounded by active volcanoes, black lakes and dense
woods, the early Greeks choose to build a great temple to Apollo,
their god of love and music, and a sanctuary for the Sybil, his much-
feared prophetess. Directly across the Bay of Naples from the
remains of the Temple of Apollo, on the island of Ischia, is another
hillside temple also dedicated to music and love and inspired by
the symbolism of Apollo and his Sybil. It is called the Temple
of the Sun and it is set on the terraces of the exquisite garden of
La Mortella, initially designed as a place of retreat for the British
composer Sir William Walton by his redoubtable wife, Susana. I
walked up the processional steps and entered through a trapezoidal
doorway. Within, I found three interconnected chambers lit by
shafts of light beamed through jagged openings in the ceiling. I
was drawn by the sounds of water towards the chamber to my left.
Here, high up in the corner above a flowing cloak of cut stone, a

sculpted egg imprinted with the delicate outline of Apollo's lyre and it's golden strings nests in a hood of speckled green glass.

From the base of this egg, through a finely carved, vulva-shaped opening, the water begins to cascade. It rushes down over the rocks embroidered with baby ferns into a channel filled with palms and on towards a small relief on the wall of a figure of the goddess Leto giving birth to Apollo as she clings to a palm tree. On an adjoining wall another small relief depicts the chariot pulled by swans that Apollo's father, Zeus, sent to carry him to adulthood.

I follow the water channel with its palms and ferns as it weaves its way toward the vaporous mists of the central chamber. Before me, on the middle wall, a huge stucco relief in the shape of a sun disc is imprinted with an image of Apollo driving his chariot and scattering the golden rays of the sun in all directions. To my left and my right the rays transform themselves into musical notes and words from William Walton's great works *Belshazzar's Feast* and *Troilus and Cressida*. An arabesque tendril winds its way around the entrance to the third chamber in the shape of the letter omega. As the last letter of the Greek alphabet, it ominously signals the end of mortal life.

A stone sculpture of the Sybil of Cumae is here surrounded by her attendant imagery. She sits crouched in a rock cave set above a stream of water, enveloped in a reddish watery haze with serpent guardians from the underworld lying at her feet. Two doves flutter on the walls beyond her, symbolising the entrance to Hades. According to legend, Apollo refused her the gift of eternal youth because she spurned his amorous advances. However, he later relented and spared her the pain of extreme old age by offering her instead rebirth as a cicada. Its image in vivid green glass lies encrusted on the walls of her cave. She is at once the symbol of death and rebirth.

I walk out of the temple into a view of the evening light playing its luminous games with the waters of the Bay of Naples.

A bank of cloud covered the face of the setting sun, scattering rays in every direction and mirroring the outline of the sun ray relief on the wall of the central chamber behind me. Two millennia of suns have set on the legend of Apollo and his Sybil and yet they live on immortalised in the universal language of human existence. There will always be birth and life and death and music and love.

PHALLIC BLESSINGS
IN BHUTAN

FROM THE AIR, THE TINY KINGDOM OF BHUTAN SUDDENLY appears from the mists of the Himalayan clouds like a sylvan paradise on earth. Squeezed as it is between India, China and Nepal, Bhutan's unique geographical location ensures that it is a verdant land of tropical vegetation, floral forests, fertile farmlands and lush green valleys embraced forever in the icy gaze of snow-covered peaks and glaciers.

This is a country where the people practice the Buddhist religion, where property is passed on through the female line, where modesty reigns supreme so that even the slightest sight of female flesh or affection between the sexes in public is frowned upon. Yet the dominant image depicted on the walls of every house is a large painted phallus, often accompanied by a carved phallus dangling from the roof.

Granted, there's a lot of humour prompted by these phallic images, especially the painted ones. They are often depicted in various comical poses, dancing, smoking or smiling, and decked with streamers, ribbons and bows.

They are light-hearted and amusing but intriguing to the Western eye. When I enquired from a Bhutanese friend about the origin of the tradition of phallic imagery, he told me that the answer lay in the legend of the Divine Madman. 'You must go and visit his monastery called Chimi Lhakhang when you go to the Punakha Valley,' he said, 'and then you will understand everything.'

So I went to Chimi Lhakhang, the temple of the Divine Madman, which is perched on a hill beyond lilting streams and terraced grain fields, surrounded by screens of jagged mountains. In the courtyard I found a lone monk of middle age, dressed in saffron and burgundy robes. He was the keeper of the temple. The Divine Madman, I learned, was a fifteenth-century Tibetan nobleman called Drukpa Kunley who became a monk. He quickly tired of monastic life and all its orthodoxy and devoted himself instead to the sensual pleasures of wine, women, poetry and song. His devotion was mainly to women, it seems, because he is reputed to have fathered thousands of children all over the country. He is also said to have made himself more attractive to women by decorating his penis with ribbons and coloured threads. It is this disembodied image that has become the symbol of fertility adorning every home in Bhutan, while the temple of Chimi Lhakhang that houses his shrine has become a place of pilgrimage. Women flock here to be blessed, and the monk took me inside the temple to show me how the blessing was done.

Within, the temple was dimly lit and sweetly scented by candles, incense and flowers. The portly statue of the Divine Madman was seated side-by-side with his faithful dog, Sachi. Both were garlanded with white prayer scarves and strings of turquoise, coral and pearl beads and surrounded by urns of flowers, incense and candles. A selection of phallic objects in wood and ivory lay beside the Madman's statue. The monk began his blessings by reciting sutras or prayers in a low, chanting tone, which continued throughout each stage of the ceremony. Then he tapped me on the head and shoulders with the Divine Madman's archery set. After the archery blessing he tapped me on the head and shoulders with a wooden penis and blessed me in the same way with an ivory one. After that, he sprinkled me with holy water and gave me a glass of water to drink. Finally, he asked me to throw the dice for good luck.

As he performed his fertility blessing I was reminded of a poem that Drukpa Kunley is said to have recited to his Bhutanese teacher Pema Linga:

> I, the madman from Kyishodruk,
> Wander around from place to place;
> I believe in lamas when it suits me,
> I practice the Dharma in my own way.
> I choose any qualities, they are all illusions,
> Any gods, they are all the Emptiness of the Mind.
> I use fair and foul words for Mantras; it's all the same.
> My meditation practice is girls and wine;
> I do whatever I feel like, strolling around the Void.

CHRISTMAS
IN ETHIOPIA

AFTER CHRISTMAS A FEW YEARS AGO, I FLEW FROM A DUBLIN
shrouded in freezing fog to the sunny Horn of Africa and Addis
Ababa to find that Christmas had not yet arrived there.

At my hotel in Addis a tourist poster proudly proclaimed
'Ethiopia – 13 months of sunshine'. I discovered that each
Ethiopian year has thirteen months because the Ethiopian
calendar is based on the Coptic or Alexandrian calendar and not
the Gregorian calendar we use in the West. Consequently, by
their reckoning, I was nearly eight years younger than I had been
the previous day in Dublin.

Armed with my new found youth, I set out by Twin Otter
plane to visit the Christian sites along the ancient historic route
of Northern Ethiopia.

My first stop was Axum. A sanctuary here in the Church of St
Mary of Zion is said to house the original Ark of the Covenant
containing the tablets of law given to Moses by God on Mount
Sinai. Legend says it was stolen from Jerusalem by the sons of
the Elders of Israel when they accompanied Menelik I, son of

King Solomon and the Queen of Sheba, back to his mother's home in Ethiopia.

Forbidden to enter the sanctuary because I am a woman, I joined the other women and the beggars at the gates. We sat under the broad sweeps of the purple flowers of the jacaranda trees and watched the white-shawled male congregation arrive for Greek Orthodox Mass on Ethiopian Christmas Day. In the bright African sunlight, under a clear blue sky, flower-scented breezes mingled the sounds of the birds singing with the echoes of male choirs and the music and songs from the psalms of Old Testament time.

It was the seventh of January and Christmas (or Genna, as it is called here) celebrations had begun. They would continue intermittently until the Ethiopian feast of the Epiphany (or Timkat), which is celebrated on the nineteenth of January. Then the Ark of the Covenant (or Tabot) and all its replicas would be taken with due pomp and ceremony to the nearest body of water where ritual baptism, Mass and candlelit ceremonies would take place.

In a land where rainfall is scarce and famine is rife, a body of water is hard to find. Therefore the city of Gondar, situated in the Kaha river valley, with its proximity to Lake Tana, source of the Blue Nile, has become the centre of the largest festival to celebrate the feast of the Epiphany in Ethiopia.

On the eve of the festival I watched colourful processions of caskets carrying the replicas of the Ark of the Covenant make their way towards the sunken swimming pool of the seventeenth-century summer palace of the great Christian emperor Fasilides. Here people and priests underwent ritual baptism by immersing their entire bodies in the waters of the pool to commemorate Christ's baptism by John the Baptist. Then they held a candlelit vigil of prayer, music and song throughout the night. At dawn the liturgy of the Greek Orthodox Mass was sung.

The main procession of the Ark of the Covenant back to the holy of holies in the churches began at midday. The streets were thronged with people; bells were ringing, drums beating, sistra jingling, trumpets blaring, banners waving, columns of silver fretwork crosses sparkling, clouds of frankincense and myrrh rising from swinging bronze censers. Music, songs, chanting and ululation filled the air. People danced in the streets. The men and boys wore white. The women and girls wore multicoloured prints and elaborately plaited hair styles. The priests wore golden brocade capes and silver filigree crowns. Their attendants carried gold lamé umbrellas. The caskets containing the replicas of the Ark of the Covenant were wrapped in embroidered silks and encased within other caskets. They were carried solemnly on biers wound with silk and brocade. Under the scorching sun, the procession was a dazzling spectacle of light and sound.

The final day of Timkat was devoted to the commemoration of the archangel Michael. I visited the fabled Church of Debra Berhan Selassie in Gondar. There I found hosts of angels looking down on me from the ceiling of the church. Drawn at a unique moment of artistic liberation from the rigid constraints of Byzantine art, these beautiful life-size portraits with oval Ethiopian features and great almond eyes are surrounded by fan-shaped frames of delicately drawn wings in tints of red and cream and green and gold. This sublime celestial angel cloud with dark expressive eyes forever fixed from the heavens to the earth is indelibly imprinted on my mind as a perfect epilogue for a Christmas journey through the Christian sites of Ethiopia.

PART THREE

TURNING POINTS

A VISIT TO THE
CỦ CHI TUNNELS

THE ROAD FROM SAIGON TO THE CỦ CHI TUNNELS WAS CHOKED with produce going to the market. Everything that moves or flies was heading for the pot, including litters of short-haired, fawn-coloured puppies. These would eventually end up on the dinner plate, heavily spiced and served as a delicacy known as 'black dog'.

We drove by paddy fields shimmering in the sunlight, past sleepy villages and vast tracts of newly planted farmland edged with groves of fruit and nut trees. This pastoral idyll is alleged to have been the scene of some of the fiercest fighting of the Vietnam War. It is said that every square metre of the surrounding area was once embedded with three kilograms of metal from the bombs of the American military. Underneath that metal blanket, in the womb of the earth, a two-hundred-kilometre labyrinth of tunnels zigzagged between the hamlets and villages of the Vietnamese resistance. Located on three levels to a depth of twenty-one feet, this ingeniously designed underground world was scooped out by hand with spades and baskets.

A Vietcong war veteran with an ironic turn of phrase and a twinkle in his eye was my guide. We walked, backs stooped, through the narrow passageways of the upper-level tunnels. These were divided into separate sections for domestic, medical, army and entertainment purposes. My guide pointed to the narrow bamboo tubes above us that served as the only method of ventilation. They were concealed on the outside by a camouflage of leaves, grass, clothes and soaps taken from American prisoners whom my guide referred to as 'the enemy'.

'The scent of the enemy was our decoy against discovery by sniffer dogs,' he told me. 'Enemy bombs, helicopters and tanks were reused by us as ammunition.'

Enemy parachutes made nice hammocks, and he threw himself into one in a corner. Enemy everything was recycled and the enemy themselves found that they were impaled on mats of bamboo spikes if they stumbled by chance through an opening into the tunnels. Otherwise they found that they were too large to squeeze through the narrow passageways. On the lower levels the tunnels got progressively smaller. They were only wide enough to accommodate the half-starved frames of the normally petite Vietnamese.

For a decade, many hundreds of people never saw daylight. Meanwhile life continued in all its varied forms: weddings, births, deaths and ancestor worship. Unspeakable hardships were endured in the dark, poorly ventilated, smoke-filled, insect-ridden and reptile-infested tunnels. In a life where the main food was soggy tapioca and the main chant of the Vietcong was 'cooking – no smoke; walking – no path; talking – no voice; coughing – no noise; and water carrying – no trace', two and a half million people died, but the indomitable spirit of the Vietnamese prevailed.

DREAMS OF DEMOCRACY

ALL WAS CHANGED, UTTERLY CHANGED, SINCE MY FIRST VISIT to Myanmar in 1990. Gone from view were the soldiers, the surveillance teams and the special forces of the State Law and Order Restoration Council (SLORC). They had all been replaced, I discovered, by the dream of democracy.

I arrived at the airport in Yangon, the former capital of Myanmar, in mid-March, two weeks before the 2012 by-elections. I was prepared for long queues and rigorous customs but found only smiling faces welcoming me to Myanmar.

In the arrivals area I asked my guide, Myo, if there was anywhere that I could change my money into the local currency. 'The bank is closed now,' he replied, 'so you will have to go to the money changer in the hotel, but after the free elections we will have ATMs, and next year we will have democracy.'

A couple of days later I was in the marketplace trying to select a few pieces of fabric from the vast array of locally woven materials on display. I found it hard to concentrate on the task at hand because I was distracted by a big black rat squealing and running furiously around a wire cage at my feet. 'Why do they keep a rat in a cage?' I asked my guide.

'Ah, rat,' he said, smiling. 'Rat was a very bad general in his last life, and now he is a rat in this incarnation.'

The large crowd at the fabric stall burst into spontaneous laughter. 'Yes, yes,' they all agreed, 'the rat was a very bad general in his last life, and now he is a rat in this life. Soon, there will be no more bad generals, because after the free elections we will have democracy.'

Next to the textiles there was a stall selling photographs, posters, t-shirts, badges and red flags emblazoned with a white star and a stylised golden peacock, its head lowered and its tail feathers fanned out. This is the fighting symbol of the Burmese army and emblem of the National League for Democracy, the opposition party led by Aung San Suu Kyi, daughter of General Aung San, the father of Burmese independence. Her photographs depicted a serene and beautiful woman with her dark hair swept back from her face and pinned at the nape of her neck with a corsage of orchids or jasmine. The softness of her image belied the steeliness of her resolve. She was, at that time, the woman whose commitment, courage, compassion and indomitability had contributed more than any other factor to loosening the strangling grip of the military junta in Myanmar.

As I flicked through these images I recalled that evening in 1990 when I heard that she was under house arrest in her home in Yangon. I was sitting by the open window of a restaurant at the edge of Inye Lake across from her crumbling colonial mansion. As often happened, there was a power-cut, and we sat in the darkness while the staff scurried about looking for candles and matches. I remember listening to the lapping of the waves and the ever-present echo of footsteps, when suddenly I saw beams of light flashing along the black waters of the lake. 'The military,' the waiter whispered, pointing into the distance, 'they are checking on Aung San Suu Kyi. She is under house arrest, in her home over there.'

Later, outside the restaurant, armed soldiers walked in pairs up and down the street. They stopped and shone their flashlights into my face. I waited anxiously for a pedi-cab to take me back to my hotel before the ten o'clock curfew. I knew that if I were one minute late I would be arrested. As I left I watched the spotlights still scanning the lake and the house where Aung San Suu Kyi spent almost fifteen years in captivity.

At the end of my 2012 visit to Yangon I took a taxi to the Shwedagon Pagoda, the most venerated spiritual shrine in the country. The car was a clapped-out wreck, eaten away by rust to the point that it resembled a colander on four wheels. I clung to what remained of the passenger seat. 'Don't be afraid, sister,' the driver said. 'This is a very old car. Now we will have free elections, and soon we will have credit cards, and next year we will have democracy. Then I will buy a new car like that Toyota over there.' And we swerved at speed across several lanes of trucks and buses to view his dream of democracy.

At the Shwedagon Pagoda I removed my shoes, as is the custom, and walked barefoot up the steps to feast my eyes on the shimmering dome-shaped stupa, which is said to house eight hairs of Buddha. Its surface is covered with fifty-three tons of gold leaf and crowned with an umbrella-shaped pinnacle studded with 278 carats of diamonds. Candles flicker at every shrine and the sweetly scented air is filled with the sounds of prayers and chanting, tinkling bells and resonating gongs.

Besides the prayers and the rituals and the festive atmosphere, the pagoda symbolises resilience and strength. It has survived earthquakes, colonial occupation and political battles. It was here that half a million people gathered on 26 August 1988 to see Aung San Suu Kyi assume the mantle of her assassinated father and call for democracy.

A couple of weeks after my 2012 visit to Myanmar, Aung San Suu Kyi and her National League for Democracy won the by-election, therefore making her a member of parliament. Their electoral success continued to grow in the intervening eight years, culminating in a landslide victory in January 2021.

During that time she skilfully managed to steer a steady political course through the land-mined terrain of the all-powerful military. Her performance as the leader of her party in the face of such complicated power dynamics has helped her to retain the respect and the goodwill of the people.

However, it has left her international reputation in tatters. Her reluctance to condemn the military massacres of the Muslim Rohingya ethnic minority at the International Council for Justice in 2019 has further contributed to her global fall from grace.

In February 2021 the electorally-defeated military staged a coup. Aung San Suu Kyi has been imprisoned once again. The wire rat cages in the marketplace are presumably empty. The generals are back in power. The torture and slaughter of the innocent population has resumed.

The people's dream of democracy has become a living nightmare. Yet, the great golden stupa at the Shwedagon Pagoda still symbolises resilience and strength. Each evening it burns and glistens in the reflected glow of an orange sunset, 'like a sudden hope in the dark night of the soul', to quote W. Somerset Maugham.

TIANANMEN SQUARE

AN AIR OF EXPECTANCY GRIPPED BEIJING THAT LAST WARM WEEK in May in 1989. The student protest in Tiananmen Square was in full swing.

Spectators lined the streets to view the endless lanes of cyclists as they made their way towards the square to swell the ranks of the protestors. Some people waved, some clapped, some smiled, some chanted. All shouted words of encouragement to the students as they passed by.

The girls wore pretty summer dresses and hats or visors. The boys wore T-shirts and trousers and were bareheaded except for the odd bandana.

Military tanks and trucks filled with soldiers threaded their way through the students, exchanging greetings and waving to the crowds.

Martial law had been imposed. Nobody observed it.

Each evening I walked with crowds of locals, tourists, soldiers, students and my guide, Tom, to the square to enjoy the festive atmosphere. The feeling was more that of a carnival than a protest.

Vendors were there in their hundreds selling foods and drinks from gaily decorated stalls to the sounds of popular music blaring from their ghetto blasters. Tea, soft drinks, sweets, pastries, fruit, ice-cream and mounds of chicken, duck, dim-sum and noodles were amongst the many items on display.

On 29 May an imposing new visitor arrived in the square. She took the form of a thirty-three-foot statue made of polystyrene and plaster of Paris. The *Goddess of Democracy and Freedom* bore a striking resemblance to the Statue of Liberty in New York, though without a crown. She stood opposite the monumental portrait of Chairman Mao on the Tiananmen gate. She held the iconic light of the Statue of Liberty firmly with both hands.

The student leaders camped around her. The air was filled with a cacophony of disparate sounds. The noise of a thousand transistor radios, out of tune, blared out the response of the world to the news of the protests taking place here. Beethoven's 'Ode to Joy', the students' adopted anthem, was blasted from loudspeakers placed close by. In the background the monotonous voice-over of the politburo propaganda droned on and on.

Occasionally, a noise similar to a gunshot rang out. People stopped for a moment, looked, listened, relaxed and continued on as before.

On my last evening in Beijing I was walking with Tom across the square through the crowds to the shop in the Beijing Hotel. A student pushed two photocopied A3 pages into my hands. They depicted graphic images of people being subjected to various forms of physical torture.

A look of terror crossed Tom's face. 'Hide those pages in your bag immediately. You could get arrested for being in possession of those leaflets,' he said in an urgent whisper.

I did as he requested and we continued uneventfully to the shop in the Beijing Hotel. There I bought a souvenir box of six small, stucco, theatrical faces from the Beijing Opera, beautifully decorated with rainbow-coloured patterns and designs.

The next morning, 31 May, Tom accompanied me to the railway station. As we waited for the train for Ulaanbaatar in Outer Mongolia, Tom told me that his father was a university professor who had suffered greatly under Mao. He had lived in exile for many years and he was very worried about the continuing protests in the square: 'My father thinks that the students have achieved all that is possible for now. They have used the opportunity of the historic visit of Mikhail Gorbachev, the leader of the USSR, and all its attendant press and TV coverage to bring the news of their pro-democracy protests to the world. He thinks that the students should disband because Deng Xiaoping and the government feel that they have lost face internationally and they will extract a huge price for this. In China, *face* is everything.'

I remember watching Tom standing on the platform as I waited for the train to leave. Tall, bespectacled, rake thin, his clothes hanging off him, a mop of black hair, a pale face, a permanent cigarette stuck in the corner of his mouth.

The train pulled out.

He smiled wanly and waved.

The massacre in Tiananmen Square began three days later, on the night of 3 June.

Whenever I open this box of brightly coloured theatrical faces from the Beijing Opera, I think of those smiling, vibrant, optimistic students gathered around the *Goddess of Democracy and Freedom* and I hear Tom's ominous words on the platform in Beijing: 'In China, *face* is everything.'

THE TRANS-SIBERIAN

'THE TRANS-SIBERIAN, THE TRANS-SIBERIAN, THE TRANS-SIBERIAN,'
my Mongolian guide, Anand, said in his laconic but triplicated
way of speaking English.

I looked with horror at the clapped-out, beaten-up, rusting
wreck of a metal shell spewing steam and smoke from some
long-extinct engine that was now sluggishly chugging into the
station in Ulaanbaatar.

'That is the Trans-Siberian train,' I said with disbelief to
Anand. 'There must be some mistake.'

'No mistake, no mistake, no mistake,' Anand said, swivelling
on his teddy-boy shoes and adjusting his trilby hat.

'Politics, politics, politics; Deng Xiaoping says Russian
soldiers must move back with Mr Gorbachev from the borders
of Mongolia to Moscow, Moscow, Moscow.'

His voice trailed away and his eyes glazed over as he watched
battalions of soldiers in heavy military coats with shiny buttons,
carrying large identical tan-coloured suitcases, swarming into the
station.

'Come, come, come,' he said, 'I have solved your problem. I have found you compartment, which you will share with a nice young man from Australia, Australia, Australia.'

He waved his hand as if casting a spell over an invisible genie bottle and a very tall, very large young man walked into view, looking even more startled than I was. Within seconds we were frogmarched by Anand into the darkest, filthiest, smelliest compartment imaginable, with soiled bedding and dirt-encrusted windows, beyond which everything was a blur.

'Goodbye, goodbye, goodbye,' Anand said with a low bow and a flourish of his trilby hat. He jumped from the train into the middle of a sea of soldiers and out of our lives forever.

We both stood there in total silence, somewhat dazed. Before we had time to speak, a small, stocky blonde woman appeared out of nowhere. She wore a tight-fitting navy suit, a pink blouse, an inch of baby-pink lipstick, vivid blue eye shadow and more make-up than a chorus girl.

'I am Irena,' she said in a loud, booming voice. 'I am your *provodnik* and I will take care of you for your journey to Moscow.'

'Where do you come from,' she asked me.

'Ireland,' I replied.

'Ireland,' my newly found Aussie companion said. 'My grandmother was Irish. We called her "Ish". I'll call you "Ish" after her.' He introduced himself as Oz. I never learned his real name.

We surveyed our new home. Clearly, our first task was maintenance. The windows wouldn't open and the door wouldn't shut. Irena sent for a handyman. He arrived promptly with a small axe. When he was finished, the windows wouldn't close and the door wouldn't open. Oz came to the rescue. He informed us that he was an electrician and set his mind to fixing the problem. A few wallops with the head of the handyman's axe on the frame of the window and the door seemed to solve the problem, at least in the short term.

Our next task was to organise our sleeping arrangements. I told Oz that I preferred the lower bunk, so he agreed to sleep on the upper one. We set out our sleeping bags as a protection against the filthy bedding and settled in for the night.

After we switched off the lights I began to wonder about the past of the stranger that I was now sharing a compartment with for the foreseeable future. Words like 'electrician', 'flex' and 'strangulation' came to mind. I could see the newspaper headline: 'Irish Woman Strangled on the Trans-Siberian'.

Besides, he was a very heavy man to be sleeping on such a flimsy bunk. Perhaps he would collapse on top of me and crush me to death. Either way, my prospects weren't looking that good. I waited until I thought that he was asleep and then switched on my flashlight to check the bunk fittings.

'Are you afraid that my bunk will collapse on top of you?' a voice above me said.

'Yes, the thought had occurred to me,' I confessed, reluctantly.

'Well,' he replied, 'if this bunk collapses, it will fold in against the wall and I will be thrown onto the floor of the compartment and I'll probably be killed.'

'That's a great relief,' I replied.

'By the way,' he said, 'before I die, could you please tell me why you are carrying that enormous flashlight around the world with you?'

'It's for protection,' I replied. 'If anyone breaks into the compartment to attack us, I'm going to smash their brains in.' It was a coded message to Oz that if he looked over the side of that bunk again, a similar fate could await him.

Washing and lavatory amenities on board were pretty basic. There was one loo and one handbasin for all the occupants of the carriage. A trickle of cold water from a single tap provided the only water for washing. The waste from the loo was disgorged through a hole in the floor onto the train tracks, which were clearly visible below us. Good balance was of the essence and perfect aim essential as the train whizzed along, rolling from side to side. Even this draughty arrangement could not suppress the prevailing odours of bodily waste matter.

On the plus side, Irena kept the enormous silver samovar filled with hot water fired-up. She served gallons of delicious tea on tap while making sure that the restaurant had an endless supply of borscht, caviar and vodka. She was the best business woman on the planet, and I traded scarves, shawls, earrings, bracelets and a lot of my clothes for enormous quantities of hot tea, borscht, sourdough bread and caviar, with a few glasses of vodka thrown in.

We travelled through the vast nothingness of a Siberia freed from its winter snows and patterned by the lengthening shadows of slim trees and triangular-shaped dachas towards the silvery blues of Lake Baikal, the largest freshwater lake in the world.

We lived cocooned from the outside world except for odd snippets of information from the BBC World Service picked up by a fellow tourist on his transistor radio. He seemed to be mainly interested in gloom and doom, and added a sober note to the journey.

One morning he told us that the train just ahead of us, which had turned south towards the coast, was caught in a massive gas explosion. It was such a mangled mess of metal, he said, that they could not identify the unfortunate passengers.

On another occasion he told us that there was a huge leak at a nuclear plant somewhere and that the winds were blowing a cloud of radiation in our direction. In the wake of impending death, we arrived safely in Moscow. As the train pulled into the station, Irena handed me a gift bag. Inside I found a decorative pewter coaster-holder for a tea glass and a white and blue cup, saucer and plate. All were stamped with the Trans-Siberian train monogram.

'A little gift from me,' Irena said with a pout and a shrug of her shoulders. 'It is not from the Trans-Siberian train.' And she sashayed onto the platform and disappeared in a haze of baby-pink lipstick and blonde, bouffant hair.

The last leg of our train journey brought us from Moscow to London through a divided East and West Germany. Trains from Russia arrived in East Germany in that June of 1989 at about midnight. They were required to make three checkpoint stops over a two-hour period. Outside in the darkness, spotlights spanned a bleak landscape of barbed-wire fences, watchtowers, concrete walls and soulless train stations lit by one-watt bulbs and crawling with armed soldiers and tracker dogs.

The passengers were awakened. All passports were collected by the *provodniks* and given to the soldiers for inspection in the dim station offices. All carriages, people and luggage were searched by armed soldiers at gunpoint. Tracker dogs roamed freely. Roof fittings and floor fittings were searched for stowaways trying to escape to the west. It was an eerie and threatening atmosphere.

The third and last of these stops was close to 'Checkpoint Charlie'. Our compartment door was flung open and a very large woman officer with endless stars and insignia on her uniform and wearing highly polished boots stomped into our carriage. She was accompanied by a tall, thin and timid-looking male soldier. She ordered me to take every stitch of clothes, toiletries, make-up and possessions out of my bag yet again and show them to her one by one. It was now 2 a.m. and I was exhausted and in very bad humour.

As she left the compartment I said, 'I think you forgot to search above the ceiling and under the floor,' pointing to both. 'There could be stowaways there.'

She turned furiously towards me, stamped her boots on the floor and eye-balled me at close range.

'How dare you,' she shouted. 'Give me your passport.' She handed it to the nervous young soldier.

'Nationality?' she screamed at me.

'Irish,' I said calmly.

'Irish,' she spat, grabbing my passport. 'You are Irish. You Irish should learn to keep your mouth shut.' She threw my passport at me and marched off with the young soldier running behind her.

After she left, Oz and I began to repack my ransacked luggage.

'That woman is so crazy,' I said to Oz.

'Listen to me,' he said in an unusually agitated tone. 'We are on a train in East Germany in the middle of nowhere, in the middle of the night, in a station lit by a one-watt bulb crawling with armed guards and man-eating dogs and you decide to take on the Stasi ... and you think that *she* is crazy?'

The Berlin Wall came down in November of that year. A friend sent me a chip with coloured graffiti as a memento. Whenever it catches my eye I am reminded of Oz and our eventful encounter with the Stasi on that dark June night in 1989.

PERESTROIKA

'THIS IS A GORBACHEV TAXI,' THE DRIVER TOLD ME WITH A WICKED grin as we chugged our way in his beaten-up Lada from the outskirts of Moscow to the Cosmos Hotel.

'Since perestroika, if I have car,' he said, patting the dashboard, 'and I have licence, I use my car to work. It is no legal but I need money, much money, much, much, much money. I have wife, two children, father.'

As if checking my attention level, he asked, 'Much family, eh?'

I nodded. He continued his monologue.

'We live in three small rooms. With taxi company I earn two hundred roubles a month … No good, eh? Eh?'

I shook my head.

'With car,' he patted the dashboard again, 'I earn one thousand roubles a month. Is good, no? One thousand roubles? I need, how you say … hard currency to shop in the Beriozka. There I find good shoes, good clothes, good beer, good cigarettes, good whiskey. You pay hard currency now in case police at hotel see us.

No legal for Russians to use private car for taxi; no legal for Russians hard currency.'

He pointed to a mile-long queue on his left. 'That is queue for shoes.' And pointing across the street to another queue of a similar length, said 'That is queue for children's clothes.' And we passed many more queues for everything from bread to toothpaste. 'You see,' he continued, 'I must shop at Beriozka, otherwise I have no time to work, only time to queue.'

We passed a large grey building and he chuckled as he waved towards it. 'That is factory for making roubles … No good roubles … No good, no good. Only good hard currency.'

I gave him the fare in dollars and as he pushed it into a slit in the leather lining under his seat, he said solemnly, 'In Russia, work hard, no life. No work hard, no life. In Russia, no life.'

The blonde Byelorussian woman at the reception desk of the Cosmos Hotel looked as if she could single-handedly defend Moscow against an invading army. Armed with a single notebook, in which all of the guests in the two-thousand-room hotel were registered phonetically so that no one could ever be contacted again, she braved the alien tourists.

'Who are you?' she bellowed at me. 'I do not know you. Where have you come from? You cannot be on your own in Russia; it is impossible.'

I answered her questions, produced my papers and said that I had been sent by Intourist, the Soviet travel bureau for foreign tourists.

'We have no rooms,' she said.

'You have almost two thousand rooms,' I replied.

'They are all full,' she said, shrugging her shoulders and walking away.

I kept my ground. She returned.

'Why are you making this so difficult for me?' I enquired.

'It is very expensive here,' she said. 'It costs a lot of money.'

'I have money,' I replied. 'I earn my own and I also have credit cards.'

'I know, I know. I earn money too, but I don't want you to spend your money – it costs too much,' was her bewildering reply.

'It is only for three days,' I said gently, 'and Intourist have sanctioned it.'

'I have no record,' she bellowed, again browsing through one million handwritten names in another dog-eared notebook.

'Perhaps you have a fax or a telex,' I suggested hopefully.

She looked at me incredulously. 'This is Russia. We are not the KGB. We are hotel and we only have telephone here and telephone barely works.' Her voice trailed away as she uttered the next few magic words: 'but I will see what I can do for you.'

Two minutes later she was back. 'You can stay for three nights, but I will only charge you for two.'

I left feeling totally mystified and unsure of whether I had lost or won.

The theme of money continued to dominate my visit to Moscow. The waiter in the restaurant of the Cosmos Hotel outlined his alternative 'à la carte' menu as he served me huge bowl of red beetroot borscht and a basket of sourdough bread. The main items on his 'à la carte' included the best black-market exchange for my dollars and the best black-market caviar at ten dollars a tin. We quickly struck a deal on both the money and the caviar.

A short time later a huge man wearing sunglasses and dressed in a suit, shirt and tie, and who looked as if he had stepped straight out of KGB central casting, duly delivered the black-market goods carefully wrapped in brown paper bags. I suppressed whatever anxiety I felt about him and the covert nature of the transaction and headed out to look at the whimsical candy-coloured domes of St Basil's Cathedral in Red Square.

The next two days were filled with visits to the monuments and museums. In the spacious halls of the Armoury, the wealth, power and politics of the Russian people shone through the priceless treasures on display. No expense was spared on the collections of Fabergé eggs, one of which contained a miniature replica of the Trans-Siberian Express, the train that had once taken me from Siberia to Moscow.

Money was no object, it seemed, to Catherine the Great when it came to buying gifts for her lovers. Especially her favourite, judging by the quantity of exquisite objects attributed to him. I wondered if they had driven together to choose some of these in the empress' gilded maple carriage – embellished with oil paintings of cupids and goddesses reclining on heavenly clouds – that was on display.

In the evenings I watched more cupids and goddesses reclining on heavenly clouds, this time on the exquisite sets of the Bolshoi Ballet. The red and gold curtain, with its hammer and sickle motifs and CCCP monograms, rose to reveal the excellence of one of the greatest dance companies in the world. At the interval Russian champagne was served in delicate glasses rimmed in gold for a mere fifty cents a glass.

I left Moscow for the airport feeling that all in the Soviet Union was freedom and change until I watched a gruff customs official rifling through my bags. He seemed to know precisely what he was looking for and exactly where to find it. As he confiscated tin after tin of my black-market caviar, I knew that the waiter's accomplice had been with the KGB after all.

PART FOUR

INTO THE UNKNOWN

FULL MOON
IN PETRA

IT WAS THE NIGHT OF THE FULL MOON IN PETRA.

The first Gulf War had just ended, but an ever-present threat of impending disaster reverberated across the Middle East, keeping the tourists at bay.

Petra was almost deserted. Nyazi, the local director of tourism, was so thrilled to discover a handful of hardy travellers staying in the Forum Hotel that he invited all five of us to attend a local wedding in the Bedouin village, which is perched on a hill overlooking the ancient city of the dead.

When we arrived, the wedding celebrations were in full swing. Three large goat-hair tents had been set up; two for the men and one for the women, the children, the food and the water drums. The women were out of sight. The children were numerous and dashed around, laughing, playing and having fun. The men milled about outside their tents wearing *thaubs* (long robes) and red and white or black and white fringed *mendeels* (headdresses), which were tucked into black cord rings.

Sounds of music and song filled the air. A man roasted coffee beans in a large iron pan over a blazing fire of fragrant wood that was burning in a clearing in the centre of the village. He gave a virtuoso display of tossing the beans in the pan, throwing them up into the air and catching them again without losing a single bean to the fire. Another man pounded the beans in a wooden jar as if keeping time to the rhythms of the music.

A long line of men assembled in the clearing and began to dance. They stood shoulder to shoulder, swaying from side to side, chanting in pairs and clapping occasionally. Then they changed tempo and danced faster and faster, stamping their feet when the leader at the head of the line swung his *mendeel* in circles. A man wearing what looked to me like a woman's black abaya jumped out of the shadows and danced frenetically around the other men. He opened his voluminous garment at intervals as if to envelop one of the dancers within it. The other men swirled away from him. After a series of unsuccessful attempts to entrap any of them he jumped back into the shadows again and disappeared. The music stopped. Everyone clapped.

A man began to sing in a loud, clear voice. More male voices joined him, one following the other in sequence. Somewhere close by I could hear women singing and ululating as if in response to the men. The echoes of their voices rippled back from the moonlit necropolis below us, adding a haunting note to their performances.

As I listened and watched, I saw a man striding towards me. He was small in stature with a very handsome face, twinkling eyes and a dazzling smile. He was wearing a long white robe and a red and white headdress.

'My name is Mohammed,' he said, extending his hand towards me. 'What is your name?'

'Marguerite,' I replied.

'My wife's name is also Marguerite,' he said. 'Please come and meet her.'

I followed him through the crowds into the courtyard of a house with brightly dressed women gathered in groups sipping tea and chatting. Mohammad led me towards a tall, blond and fair-skinned Western woman wearing a full-length embroidered Jordanian kaftan-style dress. Her hair was loosely covered with a floral-patterned scarf.

'Marguerite, meet Marguerite,' he said simply. So began my friendship with Marguerite van Geldermalsen, the New Zealand-born nurse who met and married the charming Mohammad Abdallah and lived with him in a cave in Petra. Their love story is a legend now, exquisitely told in Marguerite's bestselling memoir *Married to a Bedouin*.

In the ensuing days I visited the future homes of the new brides with Marguerite. We were warmly received and showered with hospitality by the other women. Children played noisily everywhere. The men were out of sight. The brides in each case sat silently on a raised pile of cushions in a corner of their new homes looking positively miserable. They wore shimmering *mudragas* (dresses), sequined scarves around their hair and necklaces of amulets to protect them against the evil eye. They kept their black, kohl-lined eyes lowered and firmly focused on their elaborately hennaed hands. They never once smiled or looked up or engaged with the steady stream of visitors who arrived to wish them well and leave them gifts of money.

Two of the girls were goatherds plucked from the mountains, and the third was marrying her cousin. Afterwards, as we walked down the mountain-side from the Bedouin village, I said to Marguerite, 'Do you think these brides are happy?'

'It's their way,' she replied. 'Some work out. Some don't. Who can say?'

My sisters, Anne Veronica and Deirdre, lived in Jordan during the nineties, so I regularly travelled to Amman to see them. I always included a trip to Petra to visit Marguerite and

Mohammad Abdallah. In the days before mobile phones and modern technology, telephone communications were difficult, and the mail was even more unreliable. And so my visits to Petra were largely unannounced. Often, before I had time to send them a message to say that I had arrived, I would meet Mohammad by chance riding in to their shop on his camel or driving his 'four-wheeled camel', as he liked to call his jeep.

His greeting was always the same: 'I was just saying to Marguerite the other day that it was time for you to visit us. She will be so happy to see you. Come to our house tomorrow. I will make mensef for you and we will invite some friends.'

In March 2002 a sand-laden sirocco blew across Jordan. The taxi driver was worried that the road south from Amman to Petra might be impassable. He was even more anxious that the Saudis driving their Mercedes down the desert highway towards their border with Jordan would crash into us at high speed. We pressed on regardless, stopping regularly when the fog of sand became so dense that there was no visibility. Giant brown waves rolled across the desert, and streams of sand poured in through the closed doors and windows of the car. Fortunately, we escaped being hit by the rocks, rusty barrels and other assorted debris that flew through the air around us. We arrived in Petra half smothered but safe in the mid-afternoon.

I checked into the Forum Hotel, gathered my bouquet of fresh purple irises bought in Amman for Marguerite and headed down the crepuscular Siq (gorge) in the mountain toward the luminous shaft that heralds the first view of the majestic Treasury. I walked into its light-filled courtyard and stopped to admire the inimitable grandeur of this rock-carved temple-front façade. For a moment I was lost in the mastery of the stone-carved friezes of fruits, leaves and flowers that looked as crisp and fresh as the bouquet of irises in my arms.

My reverie was soon broken by the sound of hooves hurrying down the Siq towards me. A young boy on a donkey appeared.

'Where are you going?' he asked.

'To see Marguerite and Mohammad Abdallah,' I replied.

His eyes widened. 'Mohammad Abdallah is no more, no more. He is gone, gone.'

He pointed towards the sky and rode on. I was puzzled. I continued my walk into the outer Siq, past the streets of façades, and saw a man with very similar features to Mohammad and dressed in a long sheepskin coat and *mendeel* walking towards me, accompanied by the boy on the donkey. As he drew closer I could see that he was weeping.

'Salaam,' he said, tears streaming down his face. He took both my hands in his. 'I am Ibraheem, Mohammad's brother. Sadly, he is dead. He died suddenly a few weeks ago.'

I remember standing there numbed with shock and disbelief. Everything seemed a blur. Next thing, I was sitting in a cave café and Ibraheem was pouring me a large glass of hot mint tea. For a while all I saw through my tears was the amber tea, the green sprig of mint, the deep purple irises splashed with yellow and the look of sorrow etched on Ibraheem's handsome, deeply-lined face.

After a couple of glasses of sweet mint tea, he said, 'I will phone Marguerite and you can speak with her.'

He took from his pocket the first mobile phone that I had seen in Petra.

For the next three days I sat with Marguerite in her home. Her daughter, Salwa, her sons, Raami and Maruan, and their relations and friends were also there.

Mounds of food arrived from neighbours, family and friends. It was served with endless pots of sweet mint tea. People laughed. People cried. People recalled their memories and told their stories of Mohammad and of all his exploits and innovations in the commercial aspects of life in Petra. He was the definitive Silk Road merchant descended from the peoples of the camel trains of old. He had the reputation of being able to sell or trade you anything. He catered for every taste and was larger than life, honest, open-minded, generous, witty, amusing, mischievous and universally loved.

On the day before I was due to leave for home, Marguerite said that she had not been into the old city of Petra since Mohammad's death. She wanted to visit their shop and meet the other traders there. She felt it would be very emotional for them and for her but it would be easier for everyone if she had a friend visiting from abroad in tow. It was a warm, sunny spring day. We visited their cave shop, across from the amphitheatre, where Marguerite gave me a treasured gift of a Nabataean-style silver ring with a moveable circular disc as a memento of Mohammad. Then we walked a half-circle of the necropolis. We began at the terracotta-coloured Treasury and afterwards we climbed to the bleached sandstone altar of the high place of sacrifice, with its blood-letting channels and its unforgettable views. We descended to the Tomb of the Roman Soldier with its magnificent purple-tinged walls and its triad of benches for feasting celebrations in honour of the Nabataean dead. We continued onwards past the amethyst, grey, red and ochre watersilk-patterned striations of the ancient rocks of Petra to the Nabataean tea house. Along the way we met most of the traders who ran stalls that sold souvenirs, sand bottles, jewellery, water and soft drinks. We chatted about Mohammad over endless cups of hot mint tea and cold fizzy drinks. In the late afternoon we sat watching the royal tombs in the distance turn vermillion in the glowing embers of the day.

Marguerite turned to me and said, 'The first time that I met Mohammad he took me up to the monastery to watch the sunset. I would like to visit it this evening. Would you mind climbing up there to watch it with me?'

We followed the processional pathway through the mountains and entered a vast open terrace dominated by the monumental temple-front façade of the monastery. We were just in time to see the dramatic spectacle of light and shadow play out on the architectural backdrop of this rock-carved colossus.

When the deep-red colours of the stone paled to a monochrome beige we walked the short distance to the ledges overlooking the valleys of Wadi Araba to see the burning fire-bursts of the last rays of the setting sun. Marguerite told me that it was perhaps a similar moment here, watching the sunset with Mohammad, that bewitched her into giving up her Western life as a nurse in New Zealand and settling in a cave with him in Petra.

'Do you regret anything?' I asked her as we scrambled down the 170 metres of rickety steps and uneven pathways in the short dusk to the floor of Petra.

'Yes,' she said. 'I regret that I never admired that young camel that's sitting outside our door now because I didn't want Mohammad to buy him.'

Indeed, there he was, that same young camel sitting at their front door looking at us with an imperious air as we arrived at their house overlooking the ancient necropolis.

Marguerite stood pensively beside the camel for a moment. Then she said, 'Mohammad was right. You really are a lovely young camel.'

I could imagine Mohammad in his long white robe and his red and white headdress watching us with that mischievous glint in his eye as we stepped around his camel and walked to the corner of their house to watch the full moon rising over Petra.

THE DJINN
OF PETRA

I WAS SITTING WITH MY LOCAL GUIDE, MR FRIDAY, IN THE
Nabataean teahouse at the end of the colonnaded street in Petra
sipping hot mint tea.

Around us the stone-carved temple façades of the city of the
dead burned vermillion in the glow of the afternoon sun.

A dense veil of heat hung over the necropolis like a suffocating
shroud. The atmosphere was rife with rumours of poisonous gases
floating on the winds from the burning oil wells of Kuwait. Mr
Friday looked very anxious. He dashed in and out of the teahouse
tent at regular intervals and scanned the horizon.

'Are you afraid of poisonous gases, Mr Friday?' I enquired.

'I'm not afraid of the poisonous gases,' he replied. 'I'm worried
about the Jordanian army. I heard that some soldiers arrived in
Petra earlier today. I know that they are searching for me because
I am on the run.'

It transpired that Mr Friday had been conscripted into the
army to do his national military service the previous year. He had
been posted to one of the most remote areas of the Wadi Rum

desert as part of a camel squadron. Every day in the wilderness he pined for his beloved Petra more and more.

Eventually, he was so lonely and so homesick that he jumped off his camel, deserted the army and ran all the way back to Petra.

'The army come regularly to search for me,' he said. 'They want to arrest me, but they don't know Petra or the ways of the Bedouin. When I hear they are here I run into the caves in very dangerous places high-up in the mountains where they can't find me.'

'How do your family and friends find you?' I asked.

'They know Petra. Besides, I have a postal box,' he added with an impish grin, pointing to a grid-like construction known as a columbarium carved into the mountain face above us. 'My letters and messages are delivered here.'

Just then, another young man riding on a camel arrived. He dismounted and tethered his camel to an oleander bush in the shade of a lone eucalyptus tree beside Mr Friday's donkey.

'This is my nephew Haroun,' Mr Friday said. 'He owns this teahouse.'

'Great news,' Haroun announced. 'The guards at the entrance to Petra have just escorted the soldiers back to their jeeps. They are gone.'

We drank some more mint tea to celebrate. Now we could climb the 170-metre processional way high up in the mountains before us to the monastery and watch one of the most dramatic sunsets in Petra in peace.

A couple of years later I am sitting in the Nabataean teahouse once again, sipping hot mint tea with Mr Friday and his nephew Haroun. The donkey and the camel are in their usual place, tethered to the oleander bush in the shade of the eucalyptus tree. An amnesty had been declared, so Mr Friday is no longer on the run.

Our plan, as ever, is to watch the sunset at the monastery, which is a third-century Nabataean tomb whose name is derived from the crosses carved on the inner walls during Byzantine times.

Mr Friday said that he had to deliver some supplies to his cousin's shop in the cave opposite the monastery, so we loaded up his donkey with boxes and set off uphill along the jagged stone pathways and the flights of rock-cut steps until we arrived at the clearing in front of the monastery an hour before sunset. We delivered the goods and sat outside his cousin's shop for a prime view of one of the great spectacles in Petra.

At sunset the temple-front face of the monastery becomes a theatrical backdrop for a dramatic display of the magical properties of light and shadow as they work their alchemy on the planes and volumes of the façade.

An invisible wand seems to darken the recessed statuary niches on the upper storey of the building, slowly transforming them into three charcoal-coloured squares that punctuated the still fully illuminated façade. Gradually, the fading light produces a grand finale of optical effects similar to those of *trompe-l'oeil* in reverse.

The three-dimensional sculpted architectural features of broken pediments, columns, metopes and urns that decorate the façade so powerfully by day now visually assume an illusory two-dimensional character.

The viewer has the impression that the whole edifice has flattened and merged into the monochrome shoulder of rock from which it was originally carved. Now it is time to move to the ledges overlooking Wadi Araba, where the sunset continues its trail of blazing glory as it descends below the horizon.

Mr Friday was worried about getting his donkey down the steps of the processional way before dark, so he set off for the floor of Petra. I opted to join his nephew Haroun and Haroun's friend, Abdullah, the security guard, and watch the burning rays engulf the evening sky and surrounding valleys in a fireball of orange flames. Haroun and Abdullah lit cigarettes and sat chatting.

I left them and decided that I would slowly begin the descent in the expectation that they would catch-up with me a short time later. I was well aware of the dangers of the route. At an early stage I took a wrong turn and ended up on a precipice. I was working my way back to the main pathway when I heard the voices of Haroun and Abdullah running down the steps. I called out to them as they passed close by but the echoes of their footsteps drowned out the sound of my voice. By the time I managed to get back onto the main pathway, it was dark. I knew that there were other dangerous ledges and precipices lying in wait, but in the days before mobile phones I didn't want to spend the night in the mountains without a flashlight, food or water so I continued my descent to the floor of Petra.

I stayed close to the rock face and picked my footsteps one at a time before moving so that I could check if I were walking over a ledge into thin air.

It was painfully slow and frightening. Forty minutes or so later I had reached the halfway point, which I knew was marked by jutting rocks. In the distance I heard the voices of Haroun and Abdullah shouting my name and then happily I saw their flashlights coming towards me. Haroun decided that in the absence of Mr Friday he was going to accompany me through the deserted necropolis and see me safely back to my hotel.

We entered the narrow Siq (gorge), with its tall walls of marbled, multicoloured rock soaring above us towards a section of star-studded sky. We arrived at the other end of the gorge into a narrow valley encircled by dome-shaped, moonscape mountains.

Haroun decided it was time for another cigarette. We sat on a bench here looking at a crescent of new moon creep slowly above the horizon. Suddenly a blood-curdling scream rang out, shattering the silence. It was followed by a cacophony of ear-piercing screams and shouts and shrieks that echoed eerily all around us. It felt as if we were suddenly trapped in a torture chamber filled with what sounded like human cries of agony and pain, and these sounds seemed to be getting louder and closer.

Haroun jumped up from the bench. He took a box of matches from his pocket, lit a couple and handed them to me. 'Look at the light,' he said urgently. 'Look at the light. Don't look behind you. Don't look in front of you. Don't look to your left or your right. Just look at the light.'

The screaming continued to resonate around us. Haroun kept lighting the matches and handing them to me in pairs. He took out another box and continued the process. 'My last box of matches,' he said, and lit single matches now.

After what seemed like an eternity, the screaming began to grow fainter and fainter until eventually they faded away in a distressing sequence of gasping, gurgling and choking. Haroun was still lighting matches. We stood in the silence once more.

'Don't look around you,' Haroun said firmly. 'I want you to keep looking down at the white, sandy road and let's go to the exit.'

We walked swiftly past the three tall, free-standing square tower tombs, which many Bedouin believe are inhabited by malevolent spirits or djinn, and the obelisk tomb, with its rooms where memorial feasts were held for the dead. We kept our eyes firmly fixed on the road until we arrived at the gates of Petra, which were locked. We climbed over a wall, clambered down the side of a slope and entered the Forum Hotel. Once safely in the lobby we ordered some mint tea.

'What did we hear, Haroun?' I asked.

'The djinn of Petra,' he said. 'We heard the djinn or spirits of Petra.'

Varying stories of the djinn have featured in Arabic folk tales through the ages, but the description of the features of the djinn is always the same. They assume tall, human forms and they have cloven feet. Their faces have vertical mouths and slit eyes. The males are endowed with a monumental penis. The females have monumental breasts. They appear at night and are said to scream so loudly that they frighten their victims to death.

I don't know what we heard on that night, but we both experienced it and it was terrifying and very real to both of us at the time. I later learnt that the reason that Haroun kept handing me the lighted matches was that the Bedouin say that the evil spirits can't harm you if you focus on a fire or a flame.

I also learned that the bench that we were sitting on that night is close to the site where sixty people died in a flash flood in 1963. It is said that places have echoes, and I have always believed that what Haroun and I heard on that night was a resonance of that tragic event.

THE QUEEN
OF SHEBA

MY FIRST IMPRESSION OF YEMEN WAS OF A SEA OF MOUSTACHIOED men wearing dangerous-looking daggers in colourful pouches at their waists and chewing some substance that extended their jaws into the shape of a golf ball.

I had arrived in Sana'a, the capital, at midnight on a flight from Amsterdam. My luggage had departed elsewhere – Saudi Arabia or Syria – and the airline, concerned and confused, had given me a men's 'survival kit' to tide me over. It contained shaving cream, a razor, aftershave lotion and a T-shirt that had 'MAN' written in big letters across the front. Armed with these, I headed out into the warm Yemeni night to the airport taxi rank, where I met Norman.

Norman had been fasting all day for the holy month of Ramadan. Like all of the Muslim world, his sense of time had been temporarily reversed. Day had turned into night for fasting and sleeping, and night into day for living, working and chewing 'khat'. A bunch of khat, a hallucinogenic plant, lay like a big sheaf of box-hedge foliage on the seat beside him. He tore strips off the bunch and handed them to me. He then replenished his own already extended mouthful and talked black-market money rates, his eyes fixed firmly on me in the back seat, as he drove towards a maze of headlights all swerving in our direction.

In the face of impending death I stuffed my mouth full of khat leaves in the hope that when we crashed I would float away in a drugged daze. Unfortunately, I did not have the knack of extracting its magical properties, and my chewing released instead only a strong smell of newly mown hay.

My black-market financial dealings were more successful. Norman peeled off wads of dirty notes from a huge bundle of money that he held in the same hand as the steering wheel, which by now was our only fragile tether holding us to this earth from eternity.

Miraculously, we survived. As I staggered up the steps of the hotel, Norman shouted after me, 'You will need a safe taxi driver in Sana'a. These drivers here, they are very dangerous. I will be waiting for you tomorrow.'

My hotel, named after the legendary Queen of Sheba, was of the two-sheet deluxe variety. Hotels in Yemen are graded not by the star system but by the sheet count on the bed. No-sheet, one-sheet, two-sheet and two-sheet deluxe. The deluxe option is the only one that guarantees a regular washing schedule for the said sheets, so I opted for that extravagance.

The next morning, while I waited for my luggage to arrive, I decided to venture out and explore Sana'a. An armed bodyguard was a necessity, I had been told, but the hotel staff felt that a bodyguard was only required for travel outside Sana'a, so I went alone.

Within moments of leaving the hotel I was joined by Mohammed. Mohammed was the prototype of the ubiquitous young men who want to act as unofficial local guides for all tourists worldwide. Normally, these young men are polite and helpful, and experience has taught me that it is far less stressful to let them tag along. In fact, I was quite glad he was there on this occasion, because a short distance from the hotel, in a narrow, shady alleyway, a man ran out of a doorway barefoot with his djellaba (long robe) bundled up around his naked genitals. He was shouting and jumping about me and hoisting up his clothes and gesticulating. Mohammed looked very calm and I took my cue from him.

'What is troubling this man?' I asked.

Mohammed shrugged his shoulders nonchalantly and said, 'He is mad. Would a sane man run along the hot streets without his shoes on?'

It was not lack of shoes that initially bothered me.

We continued our journey to the end of the alleyway and walked out of the twentieth century into the magical, timeless world of the ancient city of Sana'a. Crowned with a network of domes, minarets and crenellations, it rose dramatically before us, so visually stunning in the intense sunlight that it seemed a dream, like walking into the pages of a medieval fairy tale where the palaces are made of gingerbread and windows and architectural features are sugar-iced white. But this was not a dream, and we wandered through a labyrinth of tall, woven mud-brick towers inlaid with decorative stucco window arches and embellished with a white-washed lacework of geometric patterns and designs.

Life in Sana'a, founded by Shem, son of Noah, has changed little, I discovered, since the days of the ancient trade routes. Intoxicating smells of spices and incense hung like a perfumed cloud in the air and drew everyone towards its source: the souk. This densely crowded market place spilled out into the adjoining lanes in a colourful array of people and merchandise. Sounds of chatter, laughter, barter and exchange mingled with the sounds of children playing and roaming animals and fowl. Every trade had its section. Mysterious women, shrouded totally in black or dressed in colourful shawls and veils, glided through crowds of dagger-bearing men wearing Eastern-style djellabas, Western-style jackets and red or black and white Palestinian *mashadda* headdresses. At intervals, the call of the muezzin to prayer gave an ordered sense of time to the otherwise timeless atmosphere of a market place in what is arguably the oldest inhabited city on earth.

Later that evening in my hotel, I picked up a copy of the *Yemen Times*. From the editorial I learned that hijacking was a favourite local pastime. Various tribesmen had a lucrative smuggling operation in action with their co-conspirators in Saudi Arabia. The plan was simple: steal a Land Cruiser, drive it to the border and sell it; then steal another and repeat the process. If the Land Cruiser was filled with tourists, so much the better. They were detained at the pleasure of the tribesmen and returned in exchange for a new length of paved road or a new water system. The good news was that the hostages were normally well looked after. Arab traditions prevailed and guests, even hostages, were accorded generous hospitality during their captivity. Apparently each member of the last kidnapped group had gained six kilos in captivity.

Over the next few days I discovered that certain routes throughout Yemen were controlled by various tribesmen and the best policy was to hire one as a driver and guide. One of the hotel managers told me that he knew such a tribesman, whom he described as the best in the business, who would accompany me along the old frankincense route.

Hey presto, a man called Mohammed arrived in a beaten-up Land Cruiser that was way past its steal-by date. Mohammed was a small, slim, chain-smoking man with a deeply lined face, flashing eyes and a ready smile that revealed a fortune in gold teeth. He wore a diamond encrusted ring on his finger, a

Kalashnikov over his shoulder and a dagger at his waist. A truck load of petrol supplies, stored in rusty cans, were secured to the roof-rack of the Land Cruiser by a network of ropes.

As he loaded my luggage I could see that he also carried a stash of spare guns in the boot. I knew that with Mohammed I would be perfectly safe from marauding tribesmen. Clearly, I was travelling with one of their own.

We drove from Sana'a to Ma'rib past sugar-iced, mud-brick villages perched on precipices that hung precariously between heaven and earth. Below them, scalloped terraces of farmland slid into steep valleys and wild canyons, only to climb again to the summits of other peaks that tumbled in serrated sequences through the clouds to some distant amethyst horizon.

We wound our way down from the lushness of this mountain terrain to the desert city of Ma'rib just as the sliver of a new moon signalled the end of the holy month of Ramadan and the beginning of the festival of Eid.

We set out again long before dawn to cross the desert from Ma'rib, capital of the Queen of Sheba's ancient Sabaean kingdom, to the Hadhramaut valley, fifteen hours away. We stopped to drink tea or chat with the Bedouin or to fix the punctures that seemed to occur at hourly intervals. On our fourth puncture stop a group of men bearing Kalashnikovs marched over the brow of a sand dune and invited us to join their chieftain for an Eid lunch to celebrate the end of Ramadan. We did not dare to refuse.

The chieftain, a one-armed man, seated me on his left side as an honorary guest. His guards, sons and other male friends crushed around the large plastic sheet on the ground where the women had placed the food. It was a feast of vegetables, bread, rice, sauces and a huge pot of baby lamb stew. The chieftain used his right hand both to serve me and to eat from himself. He was a most attentive host, scooping large portions of tender lamb stew with his coarse leathery hand from the pot and placing it into my right hand at regular intervals. I watched Mohammed somewhat nervously to try to gauge if we were captives. The more he laughed and his gold teeth glistened, the more I felt assured that we had not been kidnapped. After lunch the chieftain and his armed guards accompanied us back to our Land Cruiser and we continued safely on our journey.

We passed the city of Shibham with its pre-Christian, mud-brick skyscraper towers and followed the old camel-train route through sand mountains and stony desert that flowed in shimmering aquamarine towards a watery horizon. Along this trade route tons of luxury goods, gold, perfumes and frankincense were carried to the palaces, temples and homes of the rich of the ancient world. Groves of gnarled frankincense trees, or *Boswellia carterii*, with their polished verdigris bark and priceless resin were scattered in a landscape of spectacular sculpted rock formations and scraggy farms.

Clusters of women covered from head to toe in black and wearing tall beehive hats worked parched fields untouched by time and trade. It is said that the women store their lunches of pita bread and vegetables in the crown of these hats, which function as both lunch box and oven in the searing heat of Arabia.

In the nearby villages the men offered us pots of sweet tea. They also offered khat to Mohammed, while the children hennaed my hands with little abstract patterns to mark the Festival of Eid.

Mohammed told me that he had learned that there was a lot of tribal fighting on the road back to Sana'a and that I would be safer to fly. On the plane I sat beside an oil rig worker dressed in nylon overalls in the stifling heat. He explained that on the previous day his guard and driver had been shot dead by tribesmen, his money and his passport had been stolen, and he had been left wandering in the desert for twelve hours until he was eventually rescued by the army.

His harrowing story confirmed for me that every journey is fraught with dangers if events conspire against you, regardless of location, but I still believe that in the land of the Queen of Sheba, the visitor is an honoured guest.

TRAVELLING THE NILE IN STYLE

'WHAT ABOUT SOME TEA, SAYEED?' ANDREW, OUR GUIDE, SHOUTED down the felucca hold.

A small figure with a moustache and a moon-shaped face emerged bearing a rusty bucket. He dipped it in the Nile to get water for the tea just as a rotting animal carcase floated by on the other side of the boat. My heart jumped in terror.

'What about bilharzia?' I enquired in a strangled voice.

'Bilharzia!' Andrew scoffed, flexing his bronzed muscles. 'You don't get bilharzia from the running waters of the Nile!'

The tea arrived, a deep brown liquid reminiscent of Lough Derg, with sediment-covered leaves. It smelt like Dettol and tasted like Jeyes Fluid. I abandoned myself to bilharzia, and so began a six-day felucca sail-trek.

It was Holy Thursday. There were thirteen of us on board the felucca – the long, narrow, traditional sailboat of the Mediterranean regions – which was making its way up the Nile from Luxor to Aswan in Upper Egypt. Conditions on board might have been called basic. You slept in a sleeping bag on deck under the stars, rose with the dawn, washed and swam in the waters of the Nile and took to a quiet spot in the undergrowth along the bank for toilet purposes. No matter how carefully you selected your spot, an undetected pair of eyes looked out at you from behind a tuft at the crucial moment or a blast of the taped Quran from the mosques made you almost jump out of your skin.

The food was prepared by Sayeed in a tiny corner of the hold under circumstances of hygiene better forgotten.

'Did you know that all fish have worms, long, stringy ones or knobbly bead-like ones?' Darrel, a sunny New Zealander, remarked casually, as I poised a portion of once-white fish close to my lips.

I surveyed the portion carefully.

'Oh, you can't see them,' Darrel said. 'They are entwined in the flesh. But don't worry, I have plenty of powders and potions to see you right.'

The choice was between bilharzia parasites and worms, so I concentrated instead on absorbing 'the local colour', to quote a well-known line from Agatha Christie's *Death on the Nile*.

The scene along the banks of the Nile looked as if it had not changed for two thousand years. In the shadow of the palm groves, the dwelling places were huddles of mud brick, mostly unfinished, with clay floors and even more primitive outhouses around them. The privileged few who had been to Mecca decorated the outside walls with the story of their journey in pictures and script. The men and children were dressed in kaftans and turbans and the women were covered from head to toe in black. In the early morning, families could be seen squatting on the ground outside, surrounded by goats, donkeys, cattle, dogs and a variety of farm debris. Silhouetted against the sugar cane and grain fields, the farmer clad in turban and kaftan riding bareback on his donkey evoked a biblical scene, while on the river, similarly dressed fishermen frightened fish into their trailing nets by beating loudly on drums.

Easter Sunday began for us at 2.30 a.m. when the first of the fifty-day winds, or *Khamaseen*, arrived. The previously mirror-calm Nile took on an angry swell and the high winds and breaking waves drowned out even the thunderous sounds of the snoring parties among us. In the moonlight, half asleep, I saw the bearded figure of Abaz, the boatman, firmly placed at the tiller, while his companion, Taleb, climbed barefoot up the mast to unfurl the sail with the stealth and agility of an animal.

At 7 a.m. we moored at a luxuriant little island of stepped grass ledges filled with lime trees. I picked an Easter bouquet of Mediterranean flowers and leaves, which Taleb then arranged for me. He sat there in a ragged kaftan, with a weather-worn face and coarsened leathery hands, tenderly trimming the stems and delicately placing the flowers in the bottom half of a plastic water bottle with a natural eye for the aesthetic. Everywhere I looked that morning, I could see the sources for the motifs used in Egyptian textile design and painting over the centuries. They were evident in the forms and shapes of the leaves and flowers, in the intricate markings of the foliage, in the exotic plumage of the birds and in the iridescent scale patterns of the fish.

After a breakfast of tea, omelette, tomato and biscuits, we docked at the Temple of Kom Ombo, our sixth temple in three days. This one housed a collection of very unsociable looking mummified crocodiles, which smelt horrible even in their preserved state.

'Did you hear the story about the Irishman and the crocodile on his wedding night?' Clive, an English osteopath, began, with his endless enthusiasm for such stories.

A marmalade cat jumped playfully amongst the stacked heads and glassy eyes as I listened to a jumble of incoherence about missing parts, wedding tackle, Irish pubs and pets.

The path back to the feluccas was littered with stalls packed with colourful merchandise. A Nubian vendor waved a huge cream kaftan at me. 'Forty-five Egyptian pounds,' he said casually. As he looked at my open guidebook, he suddenly pulled the kaftan from me, grabbed the book and ran down the hill waving it distractedly. Within seconds he was surrounded by a throng of men who almost suffocated me when I tried to retrieve my property. After a farce of mime and broken English, I tore out the page that contained a photograph of their greatly loved and recently dead friend so that they could take it to his family. The cream kaftan reappeared, this time as their gift to me in return for the photo.

We moored at a palm tree grove on the west bank for dinner. I went to have a closer look at the terrain beyond the trees. Vast, honey-coloured mountains, sculpted and kneaded by centuries of weathering soared skyward from the barren desert. On the patterns of their striated surfaces the play of light and shadow created every-changing images, making them look sometimes hard and architectural, sometimes soft and textural.

Underfoot, the golden sand had the texture of granulated sugar. It was laced with shales the colours of precious stones – amber and amethyst, ivory, coral and jade. Overhead was a deep blue sky and a hot, blazing sun. In the mirror of the Nile, the reflections of all of this produced the palette of colours employed by the ancient Egyptians in all its subtleties and hues.

On board the felucca, 'cocktail hour' had begun. Duty-free liquor and Egyptian wine was followed by roasted chicken, beans and rice. Roger and Frank, from England, held forth in Snorers' Corner congratulating themselves on having escaped from their 'old biddies'. For dessert they shared out the beautiful chocolate Easter eggs these same old biddies had thoughtfully packed for them. After dinner, joined by a hundred locals who appeared out of thin air, we danced around the camp fire to the sounds of drum and tambourines.

Later that night, the cicadas struck up their usual full-scale chorus, which was rivalled only by the bullfrogs and the snoring. Occasionally a donkey neighed or a dog barked. The stars appeared faintly at first, but as the night grew darker their brilliance provided a dazzling canopy for the felucca traveller to gaze at as eyelids began to droop. The moon gently peeped up from behind the hills in a blaze of fiery orange and was still high in the sky at dawn when the sun, in an even greater blaze, reduced it to a ghostly shadow.

We reached Aswan on Easter Tuesday, satiated by the wealth of impressions gathered along the Nile. A felucca journey is no five-star cruise, but it is an addictive experience. I cannot imagine what other mode of transport could have provided more fun and banter or such delightful companions to share both the sublime and the ridiculous.

AN EASTER
JOURNEY, 1916

THE GREATEST JOURNEY OF THE HEROIC AGE OF ANTARCTIC exploration began on Easter Monday, 24 April 1916, a date that, for very different reasons, is indelibly imprinted on the collective memory of the Irish people.

Half a world away from Dublin, on the edge of Antarctica, three Irishmen and three Englishmen set sail in a small open boat called the *James Caird* on an eight-hundred-mile journey to seek help for their twenty-two companions shipwrecked from Shackleton's *Endurance* expedition. For seventeen days they were blasted by the hurricane winds and fifty-foot waves of the Southern Ocean as they battled for survival against towering icebergs, numbing cold, water saturation, sleep deprivation, hunger and thirst in their bid to reach the whaling stations at South Georgia.

Their combined talents as a crew – the mastery of Shackleton as skipper, the Herculean character of Crean and the incomparable skills of Worsley as navigator – made this epic journey one of the greatest feats of seamanship ever recorded.

And that was only half the story. They were forced by the elements and the fragility of their boat onto the wrong side of South Georgia, so it was necessary to cross the unmapped interior of the island on foot in order to reach the whaling station at Stromness. The three strongest men, Shackleton, Crean and Worsley, set out again, this time equipped only with a Primus stove, two compasses, a pair of binoculars, fifty feet of rope, a box of matches and a few meagre rations of food.

They crossed icefields and crevasses, climbed peaks and glaciers, tobogganed down a three-thousand-foot mountain slope, dragged Crean out of an icy inland lake and trudged ever onwards, thigh high in snow, in the hope of finding life at the whaling station if Worsley's calculations proved to be correct. When they finally heard the siren in the distance calling the whalers to work, they threw caution and their Primus stove to the wind, abseiled down a frozen waterfall into the valley and staggered, in rags, unwashed and unshaven, into Stromness.

Last year I followed their journey from Elephant Island to South Georgia and walked with a small group of people those last six kilometres of their epic sixty-four kilometre trek. Elephant Island, the miserable stony spit a hundred yards long by forty yards wide that was home to the twenty-two shipwrecked men for four and a half months, had not improved with time. It was so small, so bleak and so forbidding, I could only think that, apart from their inner strength, it must have been the tungsten-blue glow of the surrounding glaciers that enabled them to live in this hostile and wretched place.

The Southern Ocean was still as Shackleton described it: 'a seething chaos of tortured water' beaten by storms and giant waves and littered with sky-high tabular icebergs. South Georgia, by contrast, was now bathed in the light and heat of the Antarctic summer. The sun shone in the cloudless sky, and the luminous beauty of the island's mountains and glaciers and turquoise waters made it difficult to imagine the hardships, deprivations and attendant dangers of that epic winter trek. However, like other travellers before us, we discovered that it was the spirit of their journey that accompanied us and pervaded our every moment as we sailed in their wake and walked in their footsteps to Stromness.

Even in summer this is a shadowy place. Nestled beneath the dark, towering walls of the chevron-shaped mountains, there is an eerie feeling of ghostly silhouettes lurking amongst the grey and gabled remnants of this long-abandoned whaling site. This eerie feeling is further compounded by the reflections of the sun's rays flickering through the dark shadows of the ruins. In such an isolated and rarefied environment, it is easy to believe that Shackleton, Crean and Worsley discovered retrospectively that they each had experienced a strange sensation that a fourth person accompanied them on their odyssey across South Georgia to these shores at Stromness. T.S. Eliot was so intrigued by the notion of this presence that he later wrote of it in 'The Waste Land':

> Who is the third who walks always beside you?
> When I count there are only you and I together.
> But when I look ahead up the white road
> There is always another one walking beside you.

LAND OF ICE
AND FIRE

ANTARCTICA, THAT LAND OF ICE AND FIRE, GLOWS LIKE A WHITE lantern on the southern roof of the world, or so the astronauts tell us. We took the terrestrial route past Elephant Island, famed as the starting point of Shackleton's heroic and successful journey to rescue his men who were shipwrecked here, sailing onwards past this tiny inhospitable spit of rock, over the wild waves of the Southern Ocean.

On the starboard side of the ship, giant sunbeams shone through banks of ink-black cloud to highlight the massive outlines of the nearby mountains while gale-force winds whipped the surrounding sea into a frenzied fury. Meanwhile, on the port side, gentle zephyrs blew as birds basked under the canopy of a cloudless sky or skimmed playfully along the crests of the rippling waves.

Beyond the giant gateways of blue-striped tabular icebergs, we found a radiant Antarctica basking in the dazzling rays of the midnight sun. We watched as she swivelled her snow-clad hips and shimmied her icy frame like a fiery siren from ancient times dancing a sinuous, timeless dance.

This alchemy of light and glare also gave animation to the decorative features of her magnificent icebergs. Glazed and polished, hammered and honeycombed, they drifted away from the monumental glaciers that had calved them like luminous cities of neon-coloured ice.

Some were slashed with fluorescent fissures of ultramarine or acid green, while others were gouged with iridescent caves and grottoes washed in a vivid range of dayglo tones. Many more were articulated by the elements over time to reveal a wide range of illusory sculptural and architectural configurations evocative of the decorative vocabulary of classical architecture. Statuary, columns, pilasters, capitals, arches, friezes and colonnades reminiscent of the temples of ancient Greece and Rome. They were all there in abundance, or so it seemed to the imaginative eye.

In the Antarctic Peninsula at Cuverville Island, clusters of smaller icebergs looked like a vast water park of contemporary sculptures floating in a wash of emerald and sapphire blue. One little iceberg had a pier-shaped platform that stretched down into the water. It was just low enough for five of us to jump onto from the small Zodiac dinghy that we used to leave the expedition ship.

The surprising aspect of standing on its surface was this quivering sense of movement. It looked anchored and stationary, but standing on the ledge we could feel it rocking back and forth beneath our feet. Lulled as we were into a false sense of security by the calmness of the spectacular world around us, it was this gentle movement that indicated the imminent danger. Icebergs are inherently unstable. At a moment's notice they explode like a clap of thunder and calve huge chunks of ice, causing great waves to rise up and swallow everything in their wake. They also have a disquieting tendency to shift and roll over, so we quickly abandoned our iceberg idyll and headed for the fast ice nearby.

There we found a rare sight. A leopard seal suckling her newly born pup. Occasionally she lifted her reptilian head and watched as brown skua birds swooped from the sky and ate the frozen droplets of milk that fell like pearls from the tips of her swollen nipples. Her baby dozed beside her on a blanket of snow that stretched as far as the eye could see. A line of penguins paused dangerously close to the nursing mother and her baby. They knew that their greatest enemy was too contented even to cast a cursory glance in their direction.

Today was not a day for death. It was a day for birth and love and life, and taking our cue from the penguins, we stood as silent witness to the wonders of nature in this vast white wilderness that, in the world of global warming, is itself an endangered environment.

THE LETTER

WOMAN WRITING A LETTER WITH HER MAID, THE MASTERPIECE by the Dutch painter Vermeer, was one of my friend Laura's favourite paintings. It hangs in the National Gallery of Ireland, and when I look at that painting now I notice there are striking resemblances between the woman writing the letter and Laura. Both women had a similar face shape, both had wide-set eyes, both wore pearl-earrings and both set about writing a letter with a great intensity.

Laura was an avid letter writer in those distant years of the 1980s, long before iPads, tablets, emails, Facebook, texting and Twitter became the normal methods of communication. She wrote vibrant accounts of her travels, her medical career and her artistic life, which she graphically illustrated with drawings, paintings, prints, cut-outs, quotations and collages of photographs and stamps.

Water was a dominant theme in her creative imagination. Leafing through her letters I see images of Venus rising from the waves, or of an Inuit man fishing with a spear through a hole in the ice, or of whales, dolphins, sea-horses and other forms of marine life.

Water was also a key factor in her choice of places to live and to work as a young doctor. These included Cooperstown, New York, by a beautiful lake; Newfoundland by the sea; and Barrow, Alaska, close to Admiralty Bay and the Arctic tundra.

A letter in August always signalled Laura's summer trip to Ireland to spend time with me and our friends and visit her favourite Vermeer in the National Gallery and her favourite island, Inishbofin, in Co. Galway. I was not surprised, therefore, to find an envelope lying on the hall floor in what I thought was her distinctive spidery handwriting. I opened it expecting details of her travel plans and discovered to my horror that the letter was from her mother, Haralyn, to tell me the heart-breaking news that Laura was missing, presumed dead. She had been on a boating expedition with a friend on the Arctic tundra and had not returned.

In the ensuing months, the search for her body and that of her male companion continued. During that time, I had a recurring dream. In my dream the telephone rang. I answered it and heard Laura's voice on the line. We had a long chatty conversation until I asked her, 'Where are you Laura?' She did not reply and the line went dead. The dream stopped suddenly in early December, four months after her accident, when another package arrived from her mother. Inside was a photocopy of a four-page hand-written letter from Laura to me. It had been found, she explained, with Laura's notes in a waterproof bag in the wreckage of her boat. Her mother kept the original because it was a last physical memento of her beloved Laura.

The letter is a stream of consciousness account of everything she was doing, feeling and planning at that moment in her life. 'Dear Marguerite,' it began, 'Long time no contact – been thinking of you a lot wondering how you are – missing you.'

'Right now I'm out camping on the tundra – miles from anywhere …

'Came by boat with my Eskimo man to camp and fish and hunt – live off the land as is the custom here – everyone goes camping as much as they can in the too short summers – hunting caribou, fishing, drying everything for the winter ahead. And just to be out on the tundra – food for the soul.

'Right now we are staying in a tiny cabin, one of the many scattered across the tundra – usually left open by the owners for the communal use of passing hunters. On one side is the Chipp river (which we boated up until the shallows got too shallow, sadly could not travel the whole thing) – banks steep sandy dirt – it curves around us on either side. The other window looks out onto the expansive tundra. Goes on flat forever, sky is everywhere, clouds ever-changing, forming new landscapes by the hour. We put our nets in the river and keep watch for the wandering caribou …

'It's an amazing and tranquil life. We have been here three days and no other boats or people have come by.

'Slowly my old life drifts away. Did I become the subsistence hunter – the Eskimo woman – wondering will we catch fish – will the caribou come close by – what should I cook for dinner – will the weather stay warm – will the river get too shallow to go back??? …

'It's something of a quest that I am on here – and there is something here … the rawness, the extremity of life, the simplicity of living off the land, the sense of being tied so tightly to the fast changing seasons … that the reflecting, the contemplating, the describing of life takes a back seat. And that is what is good here somehow. The predominance of life – its basic rhythms – being born – eating – sleeping – making families – making food – dying.'

Her letter ends with a promise to come visit us in Ireland very soon.

When I see Vermeer's *Woman Writing a Letter with her Maid*, I am always reminded of Laura. In my mind's eye, she, too, sits writing a letter in a room eternally illuminated by a bright shaft of light filtering through a window beside her.

Laura's haunting letter survived against all the odds.

Her body was never recovered from the frozen waters of the Arctic.

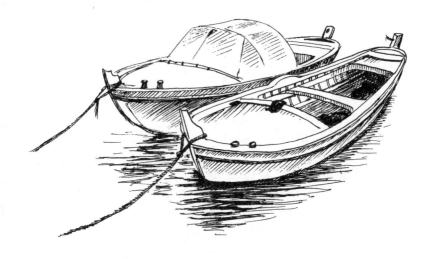

PART FIVE

HOME AND AWAY

A BEGGAR IN
NEW YORK

ON THE DAY THE AMERICANS LANDED ON THE MOON, I WAS LIVING with ten other students from University College Galway in a condemned house close to Woodlawn Cemetery in the Bronx. It was owned by an Irish builder and we paid a weekly rent of ten dollars each for the privilege of living there.

From the street, the faded grey clapboard house looked like a demolition site. The small gardens front and rear were strewn with big chunks of broken glass and masonry and overgrown with grass and weeds. At the front of the house, the windows and the door were boarded up. At the rear, the remains of a window opening served as an entrance. We climbed up onto the sill, squeezed in through the partially blocked opening and scrambled through the rubble to our various abodes.

Eight male students slept on makeshift mattresses strewn randomly around the dusty floorboards of the entrance level. A rickety stairway with missing steps and no handrail led to the top floor. Here the bedrooms were occupied by a trio of female students, which included me. The eight 'boys' downstairs worked in the construction business. My two friends and I worked as waitresses in coffee shops in Midtown Manhattan.

It was a very hot, airless summer in New York. We had no air conditioning and had to rely on fans that barely worked. A very short time after we arrived, the rancid smell on the top floor became almost suffocating. At first we thought that it was dodgy plumbing. Then the stench became so unbearable that we decided to consult the 'construction boys' downstairs.

A couple of them were studying medicine. It had to be the remains of a dead body, they surmised. A murder had probably taken place in this very house and the murderers had to hide the body for burial later. After all, we were close to Woodlawn Cemetery.

There was nothing for it but to carry out an extensive investigation of the rooms on the top floor. This would involve taking up the wooden floors, which were the only stable part of the entire building. Deep inside the large in-built wardrobe in my room they found the rotting remains of a dead dog.

Their heroic efforts and this momentous discovery were overshadowed by the fact that it happened at exactly the same moment that the Americans landed on the moon. Somehow these two events are inextricably linked in my memory.

The following summer I upgraded my accommodation from the house of the dead dog and was now a lodger in the lovely home of a kindly elderly Irish widow from Sligo who lived on the next block. I had also graduated from working in a coffee shop on Fifth Avenue to working in one of Patricia Murphy's Candlelight restaurants in Midtown Manhattan.

Here the kitchens were located in the basement. There was no elevator, so we used the stairs. We carried the large trays of empty plates, shoulder high, three floors down and the full trays of food, shoulder high, three floors up from the basement to the dining room. We, the part-time student waitresses, had a pretty raw deal. The full-time waitresses, who were mainly Irish, were justly proud of their high standards and professionalism. They had a great sense of order and routine and they operated like clockwork as a team. By comparison, we had little experience and no proper training. We fell way below their standards. They regarded us as 'cobblers of confusion'. 'Shoemakers,' they said, rolling their eyes if we missed a step. To them we were running around aimlessly and getting in their way.

Downstairs in the kitchen we had more problems. Some of the chefs whispered 'sweet nothings' into our ears and we had to be swift of foot to protect our personal space, so to speak. Because we spurned their amorous advances they gave us the worst food to serve to our customers. There is nothing more infuriating, I learned, than to serve brown turkey meat to a customer who has specifically asked for white meat only. 'Racists,' the chefs said and sent us back upstairs again with the offending food.

On the other hand, the staff food was inedible. We were not allowed to eat anything that was destined for the dining room. One day I helped myself to a piece of cheesecake from the confectionary fridge. One of the amorous chefs, whose advances I had rejected, reported me to the manager and I was fired for eating the 'forbidden fruit'.

Those were the days long before mobile phones and electronic banking. I had paid my rent in advance, and I had transferred the rest of the summer money to my bank in Ireland for my university expenses. I had the princely sum of ten dollars to my name. This was just about enough to buy me three doughnuts glazed with white sugar icing and three cups of coffee each day for a week. Fortunately, refills of coffee were free and unlimited if you paid for the first cup. Between my coffees and doughnuts, I walked the streets of New York, in the blistering heat, searching for a job. Nobody would employ me because my J1 student visa had only a month left to run and was too close to expiry.

As the days passed I became more desperate. I knew that I had to raise some money. Then I had a light bulb moment. I had seen other young people of my age selling books, jewellery and various other items at Grand Central Station. I decided to join them. I set up a makeshift stall close to the entrance with a little display of all my accessories, such as scarves, shawls, jewellery, shoes and sandals. I folded my jeans, skirts, t-shirts and tops into a neat pile and placed them in a basket beside me. I offered a free postcard and a free airmail stamp with each purchase as a bonus.

I stood there nervously on the first day. People, young and old, male and female, stopped and chatted. They politely viewed the goods on offer. They listened to my sorry saga about losing my job. They were endlessly kind. Some bought second-hand things that they probably didn't need and they often threw in a few extra dollars. They also returned my postcards and my airmail stamps for good measure.

To my surprise I found that many people liked to linger and speak to me about their lives too. I realised that every person had an interesting story to tell, and I was privy to a treasury of unexpected and fascinating revelations about their lives and experiences. I learned that it is always so much easier to confide in a stranger.

At the end of the first week my 'tenure' at the station came to an abrupt end when the manager who had fired me from Patricia Murphy's Candlelight restaurant, for eating the cheesecake, came to my stall. He was a tall, imposing German with blond hair and ice-blue eyes. A man of few words who rarely smiled. He stopped, looked at my display and spoke to me rather curtly. He told me that I could give-up being a 'beggar' and return to my job in the restaurant, which I did. He never explained his decision to me, but I heard on the grapevine that the most senior and forbidding of all the Irish waitresses had seen me at my stall a few days earlier. Apparently she told the manager that I was now a 'beggar' at Grand Central Station and asked him to give me back my job.

I couldn't have known it then, but in retrospect my experience at Grand Central Station, in all its manifestations, was to become a blueprint for my future life on the road. The willingness of people to reach out and connect, and the random acts of kindness from colleagues and strangers that I encountered there, would replicate itself as a key factor in guiding me through some of the most dangerous terrains of the world and the most difficult times of my travels to the seven continents.

Five years ago I revisited New York with my sisters, Anne Veronica and Deirdre, and our Maltese friend Carmen. We travelled by train from Stamford, Connecticut, where Deirdre lives, to Grand Central Station. On the journey I regaled them with an account of the time that I had spent at the station with my pop-up stall after I lost my job for eating the forbidden piece of cheesecake. At the exit we saw a tall, sandy-haired, fresh-faced young man begging on my patch. We were stopped in our tracks. To our astonishment he held a placard that read: 'I have lost my job. I am trying to raise enough money to go home to my family.' His story bore an eerily uncanny resemblance to my own experience here a lifetime ago.

We went over to talk to him. He told us the sorry saga of losing his job and of being homeless and almost penniless. He said that he had raised nearly enough money to buy a train ticket to go home to his family. We gave him the remainder. He was overjoyed.

As I watched him disappear into the heart of the station with his knapsack on his back, I somehow felt that a circle had been closed.

OUR LADY OF
THE WAYSIDE

DRIVING EAST FROM LETTERFRACK I FOUND THE NARROW
winding road rising up through shady pine and rhododendron
woods onto a light-filled bog plateau surrounded by mountains
and valleys and lakes.

At the edge of this vast wilderness, overlooking the Twelve
Pins, the Maamturks and the massive ledge that hides the road
to Killary Harbour and Croagh Patrick, a small church sits on a
raised stone plinth. This church takes the form of a geometrical
arrangement of masonry, grey slate, timber and glass. Its angular
outlines seem to echo in miniature the silhouettes of the
surrounding ridges and peaks.

Our Lady of the Wayside Church at Creeragh, designed by
Leo Mansfield in the 1960s, offers the perfect platform from
which to view one of the most majestic panoramas on earth.

Before the eye, a monumental landscape covered in a mottled-
green carpet of mosses and grasses and richly embroidered
with an abundance of wild flowers sweeps towards the misty
blue realms of the distant horizon. In summer the psychedelic

palette of this monumental landscape is transformed by the atmospheric vagaries of Atlantic light and glare into abstract three-dimensional canvases of ever-changing colours, tones and hues. These painterly scenes are further animated by swirls of moving shadows as sunlight filters through splintered banks of drifting cloud and casts their flickering reflections across the topographical spectrum below.

Peaks caught in the direct rays of the sun glow while bleached rock-faces etched with splashes of light and shade rise from the dark glens beside them. Rainbows hover nervously between earth and sky or drizzle down the sides of mountains to merge with the vividly coloured patterns and textures of the valleys and the bogs.

Beside the church a mountain stream murmurs softly. A gentle breeze ruffles the silver waters of the lakes close-by, but this gentle breeze can be so deceptive and its mood can change in an instant.

Creeragh is a place where the wild winds of the Atlantic meet. They are funnelled through the mountain passes and the valleys in all their fury, flaying everything in their path. A dense, grey fog sweeps in behind these storms and envelops the surrounding world in its cold, damp grasp.

At such a moment the Church of Our Lady of the Wayside embraces the traveller within the shelter of its simple triangular walls and folded timber rooflines. On the upper part of the glazed entrance wall a stained-glass window, by Phyllis Burke Gibney, depicts an image of the Virgin Mary dressed in the red shawl of Connemara, her arms outstretched in welcome. Two white doves flutter above her head and the many colours of the local flora scatter themselves in the panels around her. The purples, reds, yellows and blues of the heathers, fuchsias, gorses and wildflowers are all here in glorious profusion.

Along the walls on both sides of the church, slim, black, triangular-shaped metal Stations of the Cross display black, rod-like metal figures flecked with accents of gold.

Behind the altar a long, narrow glass panel throws an alabaster light from the ceiling onto the rear wall, highlighting the vertical and horizontal lines of the cream stone altar table and tabernacle pillar. A heavenly starburst, by Patrick McElroy, of blues, reds, greens and whites illuminates the enamelled tabernacle door. These vibrant accents are echoed again in the decorative schemes of the metal-sculpted altarpiece, the crucifix and the sanctuary lamp holder. Fiery flames of votive candles and a single sanctuary light add a sense of warmth to the overall feeling of peace and calm.

Our Lady of the Wayside is a masterpiece of simplicity and restraint and a haven of aesthetic beauty and retreat for traveller and parishioner alike. I am always reminded on my visits here of a quotation from George Bernard Shaw's *John Bull's Other Island*: 'When I went to those great cities I saw wonders I had never seen in Ireland. But when I came back to Ireland I found all the wonders there waiting for me.'

BUSH TUCKER
AND BILLY TEA

IT WAS A BIBLICAL MOMENT AT SYDNEY AIRPORT. I HAD JUST handed a big red apple to the customs officer. He held the apple aloft so that all incoming passengers could see it and spoke in a booming voice to a woman colleague at the other end of the customs hall: 'Phyllis, this passenger has just handed me a big red apple she imported illegally from Singapore.'

Everything stopped.

'Send her here to me,' she said.

He temporarily abandoned his post and walked with me, still holding the apple aloft, past the long queues of weary-looking passengers to Phyllis' customs station. I was handed over with my bags and the offending apple to the chief customs officer.

Phyllis was a very large woman with a remarkable crown of black, shoulder-length hair that flicked out at the ends. She was perfectly groomed and smartly dressed in a crisp white blouse and a black skirt.

'Please open all your bags,' she said curtly, fixing me with a rather cold look.

I opened my bags. In my hand-luggage I had two boxes of mooncakes I had bought in Singapore in honour of the full-moon festival, four packets of Darjeeling tea, two packets of passion fruit butter biscuits from Singapore, a large pack of Irish cheddar cheese, a box of Irish chocolate truffles and three bags of Tayto crisps.

Phyllis' eyes fell on the mooncakes. She instructed a colleague to bring a knife and fork to her station. All activity in the customs hall stopped. Everyone focused on Phyllis. A clear cellophane pack arrived. It contained a white plastic knife and fork. Phyllis removed the wrapping from the boxes of mooncakes and slowly slit each one in half to reveal that it contained not one but two hard-boiled red egg yolks within its beige-coloured pastry casing.

'Eight mooncakes … Sixteen egg yolks,' she said incredulously. 'This passenger has imported sixteen egg yolks and one red apple illegally,' she declared, holding up the offending items so that the assembled gathering could view them. Then there was the question of the other food contents in my bag. She confiscated the lot.

She asked me for my customs declaration form. I had not declared any of the food items because I was unaware that all foodstuffs, even those that are still sealed, are banned in Australia. She informed me that I could be sent to jail for breaking the importation laws. At the very minimum I could receive a hefty fine. She told me to pack my bags. I waited for her verdict.

Then she lowered her voice and spoke to me in a conspiratorial tone: 'I see from your passport that you are from Ireland … My great grandmother was Irish. I'm going to let you go with a warning.'

She also gave me back my tea: 'I know how the Irish love their tea.' It was my first trip to Australia. Clearly, I had a lot to learn.

From Sydney I flew to Australia's dry centre, an endless desert of red earth and rocky outcrops dominated by the startling monoliths of Uluru (Ayers Rock) and Kata Tjuta (The Olgas). They stand at almost the exact middle of the continent of Australia.

The theme of food continued to dominate my visit. My guide and tracker, Mararu, told me that Anangu Aboriginal women play a crucial role in the tracking of animals, in the gathering and cooking of food and in the gathering and preparation of plants for medicines. Knowledge is passed down through the generations of women and they learn about their country and its creation legends at the women's spiritual events or while they are searching for food. They draw shapes in the sand to illustrate their stories. She said that the Anangu Aboriginal people believe that all nature is interconnected. The people, the land, the animals and the plants. They are all part of a vast life system created by the ancestral spirits of the Dreaming. Each food was created by the ancestral spirits and some, like the honey ants, are ancestral spirits changed into another form. I was fortunate enough to be there in late September for the honey ant collecting season.

In the bush, close to Uluru, Mararu explained that her people knew that it was the honey ant season from the flowers in bloom. The appearance of the stringybark gum blossoms, the wattle blossoms and the pink Darwin's heath are signs that the honey ants can be found in abundance.

'They nest under the Mulga trees,' Mararu said as she dug them out with a hand-carved digging stick and collected them in a hand-carved wooden bowl, both of which she had made herself. The ants were fat with transparent bubble-shaped stomach sacks filled with sweet fluid. 'We eat them,' she continued, demonstrating the method by holding the head and the legs between two fingers and sucking the sweet fluid into our mouths.

Beyond the honey ants, the bush is rich in sources of food. Witchetty grubs, for instance, are a particular delicacy. They are soft white caterpillars that live in a cocoon and are found in the roots of the witchetty tree. They taste sweet and nutty when cooked. Seed pods from the wattle bush are ground into flour to make bread. Edible seeds, bush tomatoes, wild figs, bush plums and desert raisins are just a small selection of foods that can be found in abundance in the vast, dry and arid desert that lies in the shadow of one of the most mysterious monoliths on earth.

From Uluru I travelled to Alice Springs, where I discovered that Alice never went to Alice Springs. In fact, she never travelled more than thirty miles from Adelaide. She was the wife of Charles Todd, the son of a British tea merchant who migrated to Adelaide in 1855 to take up the post of government astronomer and superintendent of telegraphs. His dream was to string a telegraph line from Adelaide to Darwin and link up the Australian colony with Britain and the whole 'civilized and commercial world'.

The chance discovery by his vanguard field-scouts, McMinn and Mills, of a gap in the ostensibly impenetrable MacDonnell mountain range in the Northern Territory enabled Charles Todd to fulfil his dream. The scouts also found spring wells at the end of a dry riverbed close-by. The gap in the mountains is now known as Simpsons Gap. They named the principle spring 'Alice Springs' after Alice Todd for her kindness in sending clothes, books, food provisions and Dundee cakes from the women of Adelaide to the men working in the field.

I visited Simpsons Gap but didn't eat Dundee cake. I did, however, eat a similar type of cake and I drank freshly made billy tea prepared for me by my guide, Keith.

Billy tea is a strong blend of Australian-grown black tea with a hint of lapsang souchong for the authentic smoky aroma and flavour. The tea was originally made over a campfire using a lightweight billycan or metal bucket. When the water was boiled and the tea was ready, the billy was swung to force the tea leaves to the bottom. The tea was then scooped out with a mug and served with damper, an unleavened bread, which was baked on the hot coals of the fire.

As Keith prepared the tea, I watched families of black-footed rock-wallabies swinging their long tails over the edges of the lower ledges of the tall cliffs around us. A cool breeze blew through the red river gum trees and the eucalyptus trees. Honeyeater and myna birds sang. Insects buzzed about and cicadas struck-up their deafening dawn chorus.

Simpsons Gap has a mystical ambience of shifting light and shadow. It is a deeply spiritual place revered by the Arrernte Aboriginal people, who call it Rungutjirpa. It features in their Dreaming creation stories as the home of a group of giant goanna (lizard) ancestors.

I left the misty realms of Simpsons Gap and returned to the town of Alice Springs some twenty minutes away. There I stood with Keith on the banks of the dry Todd River, named after Charles Todd by the telegraph field scouts, McMinn and Mills. Each year the Henley-on-Todd Regatta is held here in the month of September. The locals dress up in their yachting blazers and compete for the top prize by running down the dry riverbed wearing their bottomless boats as timber skirts.

On the last leg of my Australian journey I joined my sister-in-law Geraldine in Adelaide and we set off on the Ghan train for the three-day, two-night and almost three-thousand-kilometre journey from Adelaide to Darwin. It had taken two years to complete the telegraph line, but it had taken 120 years to complete this historic railway line from Adelaide to Darwin.

Each carriage had a steward and ours was a young man called Dyson, who was heartbroken. His girlfriend had left him and run off with his best friend. He was inconsolable and in a trance. We pretty much looked after ourselves, with the help of fellow passengers. My tiny compartment was next to Dyson's galley kitchen. During the day Geraldine and I made gallons of tea for all our fellow passengers in our carriage with the remains of what Phyllis had kindly returned to me in the customs hall in Sydney Airport.

In the evening we all adjourned to the main dining carriage. Stories were told, food was shared and friendships were made over glasses of wine with exotic names like Devil's Lair Fifth Leg. After dinner, in the light of the waning moon, I saw through my compartment window a landscape that looked like salt-lake flats or sand flats glowing phosphorescent in the moonlight. These were replaced intermittently by scrub dotted with umbrella-shaped acacia trees.

I wondered what might have been out there in that scrub dotted with acacia trees and those stretches of sandy desert that glowed eerily white in the moonlight. The answer probably lay in the words of a notice I read in the park in Alice Springs. It simply said: 'Deserts are diverse and full of life.'

Out there I assumed was a nightlife where the balance between the eater and the eaten was being maintained. Rabbits and foxes, feral cats and small reptiles, venomous snakes and thorny devil lizards, mammals and beetles, kangaroos and dingoes and everything else that moves or flies fighting that eternal battle for the survival of the fittest.

SAILING TO
INISHBOFIN

TO SAIL, OR NOT TO SAIL, THAT WAS THE QUESTION. THE DECISION
rested with the man wearing the captain's peaked cap and the
navy Aran jumper. His blue, watery eyes surveyed the ocean and
decided our fate. His name was Paddy O'Halloran and he ruled
the only stretch of sea that I knew as a child, those eight kilometres
that separate Cleggan, on the mainland of Connemara, from the
Island of Inishbofin, off the coast of Co. Galway.

If the weather was stormy, I remember Paddy surveying the
sea and nodding and looking and nodding and pausing for what
seemed like an eternity while the passengers stood anxiously on
the quayside watching and waiting. If he decided to sail, he would
move towards the wheelhouse, followed by a rush of people and
luggage and boxes of freight and drums of gas and barrels of
Guinness and dogs and donkeys and sheep and cows and machines
of all kinds, which were loaded in no particular order, regardless of
rules or regulations. The anchor was lifted, the ropes untied, and
away we sailed on the wild waves of the Atlantic, bobbing along
like a cork, without a lifebelt or a care in the world.

Paddy was a legend. To my childhood eyes he was the king of the sea, an 'ancient mariner' with a time-worn face who knew every current, every swell, every whim of the Atlantic Ocean.

In later years I stood beside him in the wheelhouse of his beloved fishing trawler, the legendary *Leenane Head*, and learned to read the coastline through his eyes. 'At the half-way point of the journey the offshore islands optically merge on the starboard side, and the swell is always greater here,' he told me.

As the Inishbofin lighthouse drew closer, he showed me how to line up the prow of the boat with the two whitewashed towers on the headland before us: 'Those towers are the markers,' he said, 'that enable the skipper to avoid the dangers of Bishop's Rock, a rock which lies furtively in wait beneath its collar of foam in the middle of the narrow entrance channel to the sheltered harbour.'

If the tide was low, he anchored here, and young and old alike scrambled unsteadily off the boat, down a rickety timber and rope ladder into a small punt rocking precariously alongside that would take us to the shore. It is best described in the words of Seamus Heaney's poem 'Seeing Things', which is now on view as part of the National Library of Ireland's Seamus Heaney exhibition at the Bank of Ireland Cultural Centre and Heritage in Dublin:

> One by one we were being handed down
> Into a boat that dipped and shilly-shallied
> Scaresomely every time. We sat tight
> On short cross-benches, in nervous twos and threes,
> Obedient, newly close, nobody speaking
> Except the boatmen, as the gunwales sank
> And seemed they might ship water any minute.
> The sea was very calm but even so,
> When the engine kicked and our ferryman
> Swayed for balance, reaching for the tiller,

I panicked at the shiftiness and heft
Of the craft itself.

If the tide was high, Paddy would sail to the old pier beside the pond or inner harbour. Stretched along the cliff above, a rambling Victorian house was my mother's childhood home.

'The first time you came here for a holiday you were in your Moses basket,' Paddy often told me. 'I handed you up there to your mother,' he said, pointing to a place on the pier above a rusty ladder of steep steps. 'It was your first journey and you travelled with me. It's the salt water in your veins that brings you back each year.'

MIXED BLESSINGS

REFUSING TO KISS THE BISHOP'S RING IS MY FIRST REMEMBERED act of public disobedience.

This momentous event took place during a visit from the then bishop of Clonfert to our local church in Kiltullagh, Co. Galway, a year or so after I had received my First Holy Communion.

I had somehow established in my young mind that there was a connection between adoring false gods and burning in hell for all eternity. Notions of hell featured strongly in my life because an older and wiser friend (she was almost seven-and-a-half) had told me that if you want to know what hell is like you have to think of burning in a fire forever and ever and ever and ever and ever and ever without end.

I tortured myself every night in my little bed in our house in the dark woods thinking about hell as I repeated the 'forever and ever' over and over again until my whole body trembled with terror, and I decided that the only solution was to avoid going there.

And now my mother wanted me to genuflect before this enormous man in a funny frock and a frightening hat and kiss his huge glass ring in order to receive his blessing. Adoring false gods and hell's fires never felt closer. I moved all three stone of my little frame swiftly past him and his ring as my mother dropped to her knees muttering words of apology for her errant daughter. These mixed messages were confusing, to say the least.

Many years later, just after our honeymoon and before we got around to hanging a few pictures, my husband, Frank, and I had a visit from a nun friend of his family. She was a bird-like woman with an eagle eye and a tongue as sharp as a laser. Within five minutes of sitting on the sofa she had spotted the papal blessing lying on top of a pile of pictures on a shelf underneath the TV set. 'Aha,' she said, jumping up excitedly and pointing at the offending picture. 'You always know that a marriage is on the rocks when you see the papal blessing stuck under the television set.'

This came as a bit of a surprise to Frank and me, as we had been married for less than a month!

And so, since those fateful encounters with the bishop and the nun, I have gone on to embrace blessings in many forms and in numerous countries around the world. I have been blessed by elephants' trunks in the Hindu temples of southern India; showered with holy grains in the home of an oracle in the high Himalayas; tapped on the head and shoulders with an ivory phallus and a wooden one in a Buddhist monastery in Bhutan; sprinkled with Coca-Cola in the Christian church of San Juan Chamula in the Yucatan Peninsula in Mexico; garlanded as an honorary brother by the sisters of a male friend in Kathmandu; doused with the freezing waters of Lake Manasarovar, the holiest lake in Tibet; and in many, many more ways.

Through these blessing ceremonies with the people of other cultures, doors have been opened, friendships made, invitations issued, insights gained, distances bridged and barriers removed.

I have come to realise that these rituals have allowed me rare opportunities to reach beyond the boundaries of race, religion and language and feel at one with the great human family across the globe.